OFF TRACK PLANET'S

Travel Guide

FOR THE YOUNG, SEXY, *and* BROKE

BY THE EDITORS OF OTP
FREDDIE PIKOVSKY
ANNA STAROSTINETSKAYA

RUNNING PRESS
PHILADELPHIA · LONDON

THE CONTENTS OF THIS BOOK ARE ONLY FOR GENERAL INFORMATION.
THE AUTHORS AND PUBLISHERS DISCLAIM ANY LIABILITY FOR
THE DECISIONS YOU MAKE, AND THE RESULTS OF YOUR ACTIVITIES OR
ACTIONS IN CONNECTION WITH THE USE OF THIS BOOK.

ISBN 978-0-7624-4903-3
Library of Congress Control Number: 2012944544

CONTENTS

Otp

INTRODUCTION

IN THE SUMMER OF 2009, A PASSIONATE GROUP OF YOUNG travelers met in a Brooklyn hostel and were soon bound together by a common vision: that changing the world means seeing it. Off Track Planet was born from this vision, and through our website (Offtrackplanet.com) we began communicating the appeal of travel to our A.D.D.-ridden, social media and smartphone-addicted peers with the hope of inspiring them to give back to the world by exploring it.

We set out to create movement in the world by showing Americans the value of travel beyond just "taking a vacation." We believe that luxury travel is for people with arthritis; backpacking, with an open mind and empty bank account, is the best way to learn about the world.

If thinking about traveling automatically triggers an excuse that's keeping you grounded, let's get a few things straight right off the bat.

Money

"I CAN'T AFFORD IT."

WE'VE ALL SEEN THE BOTTOM OF A CUP-O-NOODLE, MORE THAN once. So how can you afford to travel? By redefining travel to be more about hostels and street food and less about resorts and cruises, the biggest initial expense then comes down to that first flight out of the country. Some destinations may be out of your budget, but there's no reason why you can't afford getting down to Central America where you can find flights for under $300 round trip. Even parts of Europe are relatively affordable to fly into at times. And once you're abroad, holy shit do you have affordable options. You can learn everything about tango in Buenos Aires, catch some good karma at the Chao Phraya temples in Bangkok, and get crispy brown at clothing-optional Greek beaches—all for free if you just get your ass over there.

Safety

"I'M SCARED OF GETTING SHANKED ABROAD."

KIDNAPPINGS, MURDERS, RAPES, AND ROBBERIES HAPPEN, everywhere, all the time. The truth is, America's violent crime rate is higher than that in many industrialized countries all over the world. Places like Ireland, Germany, the Netherlands, Canada, and Norway have incredibly low stats when it comes to crime. Sure, if you go to war territories in the Middle East or stand around aimlessly in the border towns of Mexico, shit will go down. Cure your fear with knowledge and simple common sense.

Health

"I'LL CATCH SOME DEADLY FOREIGN DISEASE."

REALISTICALLY, YOUR BIGGEST TRAVEL HEALTH CONCERN IS
diarrhea, and you can have a fatal case of the shits. But c'mon, diarrhea is
something we've all had some experience with. The true fear here lies in the
crap our media drills into our heads about foreign germs and bird viruses. If you
get the flu, break your arm, or just feel plain shitty, every country has a hospital,
clinic, or pharmacy that will take care of you.

Hostels

"HOSTELS SCARE THE SHIT OUT OF ME."

HOSTELS SOUND LIKE A BUNCH OF DIRTY, DISEASE-SPREADING
half-way houses, inhabited by crackheads and creeps, right? Despite what
you've seen in the movies, hostels are generally safe and fun budget accommodations that allow you to meet like-minded travelers, and where you can
exchange travel stories, cook meals, and, if you get sneaky, have the sexytime.

Language Barrier

"NO ONE WILL UNDERSTAND THE WORDS THAT ARE COMING OUT OF MY MOUTH."

WE ALL HAD TO LEARN TO SPEAK AT SOME POINT. BEFORE then? Well, there were a lot of hand gestures and noises to get our points across. You can resort back to your baby body language in foreign territory and get by fine. Additionally, speaking only English means that a good portion of the world will at least somewhat understand you. You can also tutor English to local college students in exchange for help with their native language or take a few formal courses while you're there.

Time Wasted

"I DON'T HAVE THE TIME."

YOUR PARENTS MAY THINK THAT TRAVELING IS A HUGE WASTE of time, all about getting drunk and partying (and some of it should be), but it has real value that your lame day-to-day at home just can't match. Add up your morning commute, time on Facebook, and those days you're just too bored with life to get out of bed. What's that equal? A whole bunch of empty time. Every minute of travel is a change and an opportunity to learn something new. You can really milk the value of travel—and add value to your résumé and college applications—by volunteering or studying abroad.

THIS BOOK ISN'T ORGANIZED LIKE A TRADITIONAL TRAVEL guide, and we don't spoon-feed you information on any one destination. Instead, we've split the book up into three parts. The first is a collection of oddities, traditions, fascinating events, and happenings in various destinations around the world, divided up by interests. The second section is all about the practical logistics of travel and will help you get your shit ready for takeoff. The last section is a sampling of the work, study, and volunteer opportunities available abroad to help you continue traveling, with purpose, once you're hooked.

You can convince yourself of a number of reasons why you'd love to travel but just can't swing it right now. But what would you do if you weren't afraid? Get a backpack, book a flight, order a drink, and stop being a pussy.

Otp

Part One

GET INSPIRED

REIGNITE YOUR SENSE OF ADVENTURE BY conquering the world's greatest mountains, oceans, and footpaths. Let your artistic eye wander and we guarantee you'll find something visually stimulating in the streets and alleyways of even the most remote places. Gather unique pieces and fashionable inspiration from around the world to create an eclectic wardrobe that no stateside copycat can duplicate. Let your passion for food drive you to the culinary greatness found only in Paris or the crazy-ass shit people concoct into edibles in Southeast Asia. Pack a guitar or buy a banjo, join a beachy drum circle or hit up a live show, scream your lungs out and stir your soul to the vast array of sounds being pumped through the world's bars, venues, and festivals. Party like it's your job and hook up with locals from here to Timbuktu; no matter what you're interested in, there are enough options out there to feed your desire for just about anything.

ADVENTURE *and* EXTREME SPORTS

THE LANDSCAPE OF THE WORLD, WITH ITS SOAR- ing peaks, drop cliffs, tropical jungles, array of underwater animal life, and bumpy overland terrain is meant to be taken head-on and not just viewed from a fancy hotel balcony. Feed your adrenaline junkie some quality adventure by tossing yourself into the canyons of Interlaken, carving your way through Canada's powdery terrain, and allowing Australia's Great Barrier Reef prove its greatness by slapping on a wetsuit and going to town. Leave no stone unturned, no mountain unscaled, and find that next level of thrill by expanding your adventures worldwide. Everyone knows that adrenaline pumps hardest in unfamiliar territory.

Australia

REEFER MADNESS

THE LARGEST STRUCTURE ON

the planet made entirely by living organisms, the Great Barrier Reef (GBR) is a live seafood soup filled with crazy-looking and endangered animals swimming at you from all angles. A UNESCO World Heritage site, this reef is home to 1,500 species of fish. Throw some scuba gear on and discover what makes this reef so great.

Scuba

The GBR stretches 1,600 miles along the Queensland coast in the Coral Sea, and the best way to experience it is to submerge yourself deep into its crevices.

Eighty-pound grouper cruise by, schools of barracuda eye you cautiously, reef shark silhouettes loom in the distance, sea turtles float by drunk

on life, and Nemo feverishly defends his nest all around a reef of hard and soft coral that no box of Crayola could ever color-code. There are countless ways to see these billions of coral polyps. Here's a short list to get you bright-eyed:

CAIRNS

This scuba capital of Australia has no shortage of tour agencies to get you to the reef. Shop around to avoid rip-offs or book at a recommended hostel. The GBR is a long boat ride from Cairns, so an overnight trip is the best way to see it. You can get two days with three dives each (including a night dive) with food and lodging on a live-aboard boat for about $350. Some of the bigger boats feel like a touristy assembly line, so check boat reviews online before paying.

SS YONGOLA WRECK DIVE

One hundred years ago, the SS Yongola passenger ship disappeared in a cyclone, along with all 122 people on board. This football field-size mass grave quickly became a cushy new underwater neighborhood, gentrified by the swankiest of fish. Local dive shops claim you see more species of fish on this one wreck dive than you do in ten dives anywhere else on the reef.

SHARK-FEEDING DIVE

If you do a weeklong live-aboard jaunt out to the Osprey Reef, you'll see the best collections of the reef's sharks, especially when the dive ops

run a shark-feeding dive at North Horn. Dozens of gray sharks, silvertips, and sometimes hammerheads and tiger sharks circle overhead and bolt past you for giant chunks of the provided fish carcasses. Try not to crap your wetsuit.

TOO LEGIT, TOO LEGIT TO QUIT

While it's not as cheap as Asia or Central America, you can get certified to dive anywhere along the reef. (Cairns cranks out more certifications than anywhere else in the world.) As a bonus, your four certification dives are actually at the GBR, as opposed to in some Midwest rock quarry. Snorkeling is a decent consolation if you can't dive. But it'll feel like a threesome gone wrong as you'll just be looking at the reef rather than being a part of it.

Skydiving

The GBR is visible from space. Don't take our word for it—head up that way and see for yourself. Instead of squinting through a tiny airplane window, jump out of that bad boy for a better view. As wind relentlessly pummels your face and howls past your ears, you'll hit terminal velocity in a sixty-second free fall that'll seem like a lifetime. Once you're jolted to a stop with the release of your chute, you'll feel suspended in midair, soaking up the views of this world wonder.

The Great Barrier Reef is almost the size of Texas. It's not Bush country though—in fact the reef's residents are pretty pissed that Dubya's environmental policies shat all over their home. Already called the "So-So Barrier Reef," the GBR is slowly dying. Get there before it's gone.

Bolivia

PACK YOUR MACHETE, THINGS ARE ABOUT TO GET WILD

THE AMAZON IS A PORTAL TO a mysteriously green world unlike anything you've ever imagined. Covering 2.3 million square miles across nine countries, here you can learn how to suck drinking water from vines and how to tell the difference between tree bark that kills and bark that's rumored to cure cancer. You'll cook over an open fire, spice up lunch with coconut-flavored grubs, and wash it down with mint-flavored ants.

The Spread

The vast majority of the jungle is in Brazil, but digging through greenery there is fannypacker-heavy and, consequently, more expensive. Cheaper and farther off the gringo trail, the Bolivian Amazon is concentrated in the northeast of the country. There are forty-six indigenous tribes in and around the 7,320-square-mile Madidi National Park—most of which is closed off to tourism. To get there, hop a flight from La Paz to the small airport in Rurrenabaque, or risk a twenty-four-hour bus ride on the world's most dangerous road.

Jungle Booking

Rurrenabaque is a little like the American Wild West, a tiny dusty town without an ATM where locals wear a jaguar tooth as a badge of pride. It's

We Dare You Not to Die: Bolivia's Death Road

FLYING DOWN THE SIDE OF an 11,800-foot mountain—the world's most dangerous road, the Highway of Death or *Camino de la Muerte*—is part sightseeing, part adventure, part death wish, and all completely bad ass. Hop on a bike and try your hand at staying alive.

The road starts at an icy Andean summit and skids to a halt in the steamy Amazonian Yungas. The gravel will kick you in the face as you narrowly grab hairpin curves. The handlebars will shake, but tell fear to fuck itself. You'll whiz past grazing llamas, jaw-dropping cliff sides, and a drug checkpoint. Better settle for a *Huari* beer on the bus back to La Paz, but you'll have earned it. Barreling down a mountain at sixty miles per hour is as sweaty and exhilarating as it sounds.

For less than $100, agencies in La Paz can hook you up with wheels, gear, a guide, and perks like free lunch and a post-ride swim. When you're choosing an agency, remember that the cheaper the tour, the cheaper your equipment, and the bigger your balls must be to make up for it. Over the years, about twenty cyclists never got to the swim. But thousands more have given risk the middle finger and now sport a "I'm a Death Road Survivor" T-shirt as a symbol of their rite of passage. With a little panache and good form, you can easily kick this road to the curb—and live to tell the story.

also where intrepid travelers hook up with true jungle men to go in deep. It's almost sure death—not to mention illegal—to go exploring alone. The state minimum for a trip is a cool Bs 300 (about $45) per person per day, a small price to play Tarzan. You can book a trip through one of the many agencies that line the streets of Rurrenabaque. Most offer packages that include sit-down meals and a hammock at one of the several eco-lodges in Madidi. Lush mountains and rolling banana plantations surround the park, and you'll get there by a two-hour boat ride from town.

Hacking It Alone

If you're looking to head out with just a guide and the pack on your back, some agencies offer more rugged trips. A couple offer full-on survival courses where you brave it with nothing but a machete and iodine tablets.

You will learn how to feed yourself in the wild, sleep with one eye open, and stand your ground in jungle confrontations (since most anacondas aren't familiar with dismissive phrases like "fuck off"). It's important to figure out what type of experience you want to have and ask as many questions as it takes to find the right guide or tour company.

If you want to bushwhack your way through the muddy brush, pick up a machete at one of the many hardware stores in town. And the bugs are brutal—stock up on DEET to keep the bites at bay.

Five Animals
You've Never Heard Of

THE AMAZON IS LIKE A mystery grab bag of life, and when you reach in, sometimes you pull out a regular old toucan and other times, a fistful of fish with wings, floppy-eyed frogs, and plants with feelings (if you are lucky enough to keep your hand while fiddling around in the Amazon bag, that is). Here are just a few animals that live in the world's most cryptic jungle:

1. Emperor Tamarin—This guy would be tough competition come Mo-vember.

2. Wood-Eating Catfish—He may have been out of the office when all the other catfish got the "you're not a beaver" memo.

3. T-Rex Leech—The dinosaur of bloodsuckers, this leech is very well endowed when it comes to teeth and unfortunately, very poorly endowed when it comes to the parts that matter.

4. Skydiving Ant—While ants can do all kinds of crazy things (kill you, for one), this species decided to up the ante by developing the ability to sky-dive using its ass for counterbalance. Now if it could film itself doing tandem jumps with ants too scared to take the plunge alone, we'd be pretty impressed.

5. Hoatzin—People call him the "stinkbird" because he smells like manure. As backpackers, we fully understand. We'd probably share a hostel dorm with him, go out for drinks a few times, and make him drunken pasta in the hostel kitchen before noticing any odor irregu-larities.

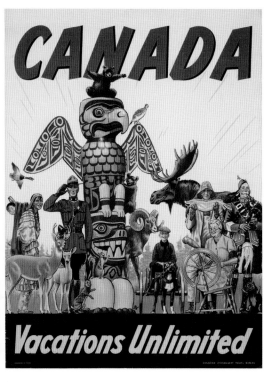

WHISTLE WHILE YOU CARVE: SNOWBOARDING VANCOUVER

THE HOLY BEHEMOTH OF North American mountains, Whistler Blackcomb of British Columbia is often regarded as the greatest snow resort in the world and is the place to put your shred sled to the test. Clip in your boots and carve a deep trail down these twin mondo mountains.

Coming Down the Mountains

With over 8,000 combined acres of boardable trails, the Whistler and Blackcomb mountains ensure that even the most serious of you snow-bums will be happily bombing down the slopes all season long. Dozens of lifts lead to the 200-plus trails of fresh Vancouver snow canvases that await your craftsmanship. Carve your tightest S's and master your jump turns down Blackcomb's world-rated "Couloir Extreme"—a fifty-two degree test of how much hell you're willing to put your thighs through. Get tricky on the mountain's Olympic-size superpipe, or head over to Whistler and race through the "Peak-to-Creek" perimeter tour trail of over four miles! Can't decide which mountain you want to tear up today? Get on the "Peak 2 Peak" gon-dola (*ganjala*, for you multitaskers), a record-breaking scenic ride of a life-time that connects Blackcomb and Whistler together.

BUM A CUP OF KICKASS FROM our North American neighbor. Knock on Vancouver's door on your way to Whistler Blackcomb, a monstrous snow resort that you can carve up until your lungs turn purple. Head down the street to Banff and load your ear canals with whitewater. And finally, get gluttonous in Quebec, the birthplace of the inevitable food coma, better known as "poutine." This continental colossus spills adventure from every angle, with both winter and summer adrenaline-loaded adventures, just waiting to be manhandled.

UNCHILL YOUR NIPS WITH POUTINE

SOFTEN UP YOUR SHIRT-
piercing nips with Canada's trifecta of fat. Quite possibly Quebec's greatest contribution to the planet in all of human history, poutine is a big ol' ball of cholesterol that can kill lesser men ill-prepared for its addicting glory. With globs of fatty juices and dripping in sticky goo, somewhere beneath its artery-clogging exterior is a Canadian treat that warms you to the core.

Pou-natmony

It consists of three ingredients, piled on top of one another: (1) French fries, (2) gravy, and (3) cheese. The fries are piping hot, golden, and somehow still crispy despite the gravy that covers them. As thick and sweet as jelly, the gravy kicks KFC further into the tunnel of shame. And the cheese? Little nuggets of smooth dairy deliciousness melt into the pile and make little squeaky sounds with every bite. Since just reading the ingredients will make you fatter, it is truly a wonder how Canada's morbid obesity rates are so low. What's more,

poutine is normally just a side dish to a main meal! You can essentially get the stuff anywhere across the country, short of Indian restaurants, from 8 a.m. to 3 a.m. most days.

WHITEWATER RAFTING IN BANFF

THE BANFF REGION OF ROCKY
Alberta, Canada, is notorious for its world-class whitewater and ferocious river rapids. A wise group of travelers (we) once said that the best way to know your mountainous surroundings is to raft right through them. Grab your oars and hold on tight—we're gonna get you all Banff-ed and bothered.

Down Shit's Creek—with a Paddle

Sometimes closed off to commercial rafting companies and always gushing with dangerously extreme levels of rapids, the Kicking Horse is the only river around here really worth paddling. The river carves right through Kicking Horse Canyon in three tiers: upper, middle, and lower. Naturally, the upper canyon (and the beginning of your trip) is friendly enough to find your groove. Miles downriver, the Portage and Shotgun rapids will quickly awaken the extremist in you. From here on, the fun and games morph into panic and survival; the bottom of the middle canyon and entire lower canyon are filled with challenging rapids that often arrive unannounced. Totaling

over twenty miles, with a consistent water temperature just above freezing, Kicking Horse River will quickly put some commendable rafting experience under your belt.

Keep It Classy

As you progress downriver, you'll start holding onto your oar for dear life (as you should) while smacking into Class III and IV+ Rapids. What do these numbers mean? Quite simply, an association of all things adventurous decided to make an internationally recognized scale of how badly the water will kick your ass—aptly named the "International Scale of River Difficulty." The scale divides rapids into classes from I through VI; I being a leisurely bitch paddle over waves that wouldn't disrupt a snorkeler's breathing; VI being a green-conscious government's alternative to the electric chair—almost certain death. Just so you know what you're diving into, the lower part of the Kicking Horse, starting with Portage and Shotgun rapids, are rated a consistent III to IV and can rush to a V during unpredictable parts of the sport's summer season. If you've got the rapids in a chokehold and your adventurous side needs more of a tickle, ask your guides to let you swim once the tour is over. Trying to backstroke down an icy-cold Class III rapid should sufficiently fire up your veins.

From mild to wild, the Kicking Horse River is easily the toughest route through the canyon. Take a one-day tour down or split the trip into a multiday excursion. However you plan to paddle, once you reach the bottom, we guarantee you'll feel like you're on top of the world.

India

RICKSHAW RUN

INDIA'S 1.2-MILLION-SQUARE- mile landscape is jammed to the brim with people, color, sounds, ruins, pungent smells, and cows. To navigate through the randomly moving madness, India has chosen the almighty rickshaw as its national mode of transport. The screeching horns of these wobbly three-wheeled, seven-horsepower mini covered wagons—decorated with enough kitsch to plaster the Taj Mahal—can be heard from Sikkim to Kerala. As common as curry, one of these bumpin' taxis can be flagged down on a dirt road in the middle of nowhere. The moment you set foot in a rickshaw and your stomach starts churning from the nerve shattering ride, you'll fully understand that every injury-free ride is the collaborative work of Jesus, Buddha, Allah, Confucius, and at least a couple X-men. Okay, ready to race one of these janky things across India?

The Run

Since 2006, crazy motherfuckers known as "The Adventurists" have put on the "Rickshaw Run." The idea is to sup-up one of these tricycles of death and race it from one side of India to the other, stopping only for local cricket matches, maintenance, and liters of Kingfisher. Your chances of capsizing, crashing, or sputtering out are pretty damn good, but there's no doubt that your Indian odyssey will kick the shit out of any monkey-petting trip your friend did. You and up to three daredevil teammates can sign up and score a licensed rickshaw for about $2,000. The annual event is held over the course of two weeks, once in summer (our winter) and once in winter (our summer). Spots fill up a year in advance, so plan accordingly.

Wait, Why the Fuck Is This a Good Idea?

Participating in an event like this takes you where no bus, train, or plane can go. You'll be pedal-to-the-metal through some of India's grittiest, prettiest, and most surprising locales. It takes mad skills to fix a rick', and you'll learn them from the country's greasiest badasses. Also, it's not every day that locals see a foreigner barreling through town in a rickshaw. The novelty can be your ticket to anything from meals to wedding proposals.

Put Some Switches on It!

While it's sweet to 'shaw your way across the country, it's not "The Rickshaw Run" if the vehicles aren't tricked out in crazy-as-fuck designs. Participants send images or ideas to pimp their 'rick in advance, and when they show up to compete, they're given the rickshaw of their dreams. It's mandatory to go for a test drive three days before the event to learn how to handle the beast, and dummy crashing it to test out that helmet mom made you pack isn't a bad idea. Once the race begins, you're on your own to figure shit out.

Need More Convincing?

The Adventurists put on a slew of insane events in addition to the Rickshaw Run, from Indonesia to Mongolia to Peru. Each one begins and ends with a party that would make Genghis Khan blush, and all participants are VIP.

The Rickshaw Run isn't only fun and (deadly) games. As soon as you start your engine, you're raking in the dough for charities across the world. In the past years, these events have raised nearly $6 million. Every team is responsible for raising money, and the funds will often be distributed directly to the villages you'll pass through on the run. This means that the same kid who kicked your ass at cricket could learn to read this year because you were crazy enough to ride a rickshaw through his town.

Running AT the Bulls

WANT TO JUST KEEP DOING crazy things after you throw the rickshaw in park? While people in Pamplona are all about running away from the bulls, in India, running at the bulls is the name of the game. Jallikattu is a bull-taming game that dates back 3,500 years. In ancient Tamil Nadu, the sport was known as "hugging the bull," though there's nothing loving about it. "Be gored or be spared" is the mantra of many a brave/stupid Jallikattu participant at the Harvest Festival of Pongal, held every year in the middle of January. The goal of the main event is to chase down a pissed-off bull unarmed and grab the bundles of money tied to its horns. Back in the day, kings and chieftains determined the worthiness of their daughter's prospective grooms by seeing if they could survive this blood sport. The event was made illegal a while ago, but the Tamil Nadu government has since lifted the ban in exchange for increased animal screenings and the promise of ambulances on site.

Interlaken

CRACKS AND CREVICES: CANYONING THROUGH INTERLAKEN

CANYONING IS ONE OF THE most extreme sports out there. The concept is simple: use all means necessary to reach the bottom of a canyon. The execution is difficult: you'll have to rappel, slide, climb, jump, and dive to make it out alive. Once you're in this bitch, there's no pulling out. You can't just roll down a canyon anywhere there's a crack. The conditions must be just right, and in Interlaken, you'll find the perfect balance of steep cliffs, big drops, and roaring waterfalls.

Start From the Top

Jagged rocks, unimaginable heights, freezing-cold streams, and no sign of immediate escape are what Interlaken has to offer. So why would anybody voluntarily do this? Because it makes you feel alive, and you can only do it (and survive) in a few places around the globe. Canyoning (known in the United States as canyoneering) has been around for thousands of years but not always as a sport. Originally, Native Americans found refuge, shelter, and food in the deep granite and sandstone canyons of America's west coast. It wasn't until the 1960s that death-wish adventurers started exploring the ins and outs of Mother Nature's deep, gushing crevices for sport.

What Goes Down

In Interlaken, your adventures in the canyon begin at the top of a mountain. You'll first change into protective gear and receive some brief safety guidelines (i.e., don't jump off any fifty-foot cliffs without first telling a guide), then you'll hike for a good half hour until you really feel alone in the canyon; that's when the fun begins. The first dive into the freezing mountain water effectively evaporates whatever balls you have left from the provided nut-hugging wetsuit. The next three hours consists of jumping, diving, rappelling, sliding, swimming, and shivering down the canyon with a small group of as-crazy-as-you comrades. It's an adventure of a lifetime, so you better be prepared. Tuck in your elbows as you go down nature's own paved slides; they're gonna get bumpy. Keep your knees bent on the cliff jumps; the landing pools can be shallow (remember to canyonball). Don't fuck with your carabiners; rappels are a long way down. Bring a towel; you're gonna get soaked. And definitely buy the individually edited HD video; nobody's ever gonna believe you did this.

Choose Your Canyon

Interlaken knows your time and budget are limited, so your choices are simplified thanks to three organizations—Interlaken Adventure, Outdoor Interlaken, and Alpin Center. All three offer similar rates of around $200 for the trip. Since each company specializes in one specific canyon, choosing your package depends on which canyon you decide to conquer. Some are smaller and shorter, others are terrifyingly large. If you want to go for the biggest and baddest, choose Chli Schliere. Enclosed in tight rock walls over 300 feet tall and defined by huge waterfalls, these are the tallest jumps and slides in the region. With extremely challenging 100-plus-foot rappels, this thing will quickly show you what real canyoning is all about.

Peru

MUCHO MACHU PICCHU

NO ONE KNOWS EXACTLY

why it's there, how it was built, or what type of magic it can harness, but a trip to South America is incomplete without a climb to Machu Picchu. The world is full of over-hyped tourist spots; this isn't one of them. This massive Incan complex solidly deserves its title as one of the New Seven Wonders of the World. Just sixty miles north of Cusco, Peru, the capital city is where the mind-blowing pilgrimage begins. Get there by flying into Alejandro Velasco Astete International Airport, by bus, or big pimp it and float into Peru via the Amazon.

OTP TIP: Machu Picchu sits between two mountain peaks—Huayna Picchu and Machu Picchu Montaña. Uncrust your eyes before dawn to see the clouds rising over the ancient complex from atop either peak. You can hire a guide at the park entrance should you need some early morning trekking assistance.

Why Wonder?

American explorer Hiram Bingham found more than 100 skeletons when a local boy led him to the complex in 1911.The Incans had mysteriously constructed 140 temples, mausoleums, vaults, and houses out of giant stones with their bare hands, right into steep Andean slopes.

No one knows why the city was abandoned thousands of years ago (nor can anyone determine what Bingham was doing following little boys around). Some people think aliens built it to bring civilization to man, and others believe its structures form a psychedelic astrological calendar.

Trek It Out

While Machu's downfall is shrouded in mystery, one thing is known for sure: The Incans didn't fuck around when it came to stairs. Any real trip to Machu Picchu includes 100 or so flights of uneven stone stairs to get to the complex entrance. If that doesn't set your ass on fire, you can also do a three-to-five-day trek along the Urubamba River to fully earn the insane view. The Incan Trail is tried and true, and a spot on an organized trek with any number of agencies in Cusco will run you about $500 to $600. Prices include park entrance, a tent, food, a Peruvian

Float Your Way Out

IF YOU'VE HAD YOUR FILL OF MOUNTAINS IN PERU, CHANGE UP the scenery by hitching a ride to Brazil via the Amazon. Much more scenic than a cloudy plane ride, the Amazon is over 4,000 miles long, can be up to twenty-five miles wide, and is filled with plants and animals even Wikipedia has a hard time describing. The major artery of South America's heart, the Amazon is sometimes the only road that connects points A and B. You can pay for a bus or a flight to get to the jungle, or milk it like a jaguar cub and get there for free. All it takes are some courage and sea legs.

guide who knows his shit, and a donkey to carry yours.

Everyone has seen the played-out pictures of Machu Picchu by now. But no picture can capture the crispness of Peruvian mountain air, the size and scale of the complex, and the deserved soreness raging through your body the next day.

OTP TIP: Ditch the crowd all together and tame those mountains with a map and sheer willpower. You don't need a permit to do the Salkanty or Choquequirao trails *sin guia* and the donkeys could use a breather.

The Road Less Traveled

The most-traveled route on the Amazon is from Iquitos, Peru, to Manaus, Brazil, with a connection in Leticia, Colombia. These rivers are technically tributaries of the Amazon,

which begins for real in Manaus, but have plenty of piranhas, pink dolphins, tiny ports, and jungly shores to keep your senses occupied en route.

Get on a Boat, Bitch!

Prep your Spanish sailor lingo and stroll on up to the port in Iquitos, flex your guns and tell them how you "worked on your uncle's sailboat that one summer." Though some boats ferry up to 600 passengers, they're primarily cargo ships that carry anything from TVs and sound systems to chickens and grains. You'll probably sacrifice your back for several days hauling cargo, but if you know your rice and beans, weaseling your way into the kitchen may be an option.

Chillin' on one of these boats is an experience that romantically sits somewhere between a no-holds-barred jungle safari and an eighteenth-century prison ship. Catch some gnarly bugs, learn a couple samba moves, and drink your way into a mariachi sunset. You will sleep in a hammock on the deck and love every moment of your successful labor-for-travel trade.

Scotland

HIKE UP YOUR KILT: AN EXTREME STROLL THROUGH SCOTLAND

A NATION THAT NORMALLY lets it all hang out, Scotland has many best-kept secrets, one of which is the ninety-six-mile hike through Rob Roy country along the West Highland Way (WHW). The "Way" begins in Milngavie (pronounced Mul Guy) just north of Glasgow and ends in downtown Fort William at a statue of a man rubbing his tired Scottish feet. The trek will take you through Grimm's fairy tale–like forests, around the banks of bonnie Loch Lomond, up steep and rocky hillsides, across farms with curious sheep, and deep into the eerie and isolated Rannoch Moor.

The Way

Most trekkers head out in May when the weather is best, the baby lambs are rambunctious, and the midges (small mosquito-y bugs that swarm and bite the bloody hell out of you) aren't prevalent. For a more extreme trek, schedule your hike in the winter with gale-force winds and snowdrifts that obscure the path. An ice pick, instead of a hippie walking stick, is recommended during this time.

If hiking ninety-six miles isn't enough, you can tack on another crazy seventy-nine miles along the Great Glen Way and cuddle with the Loch Ness Monster, who presumably hangs out in Inverness, the hike's endpoint. There are also plenty of day trips along the way, such as climbing Ben Nevis and Ben Lomond, as well as several other *munros* (a Scottish mountain with a height over 3,000 feet).

with a view overlooking the eastern shores of Loch Lomond. The food tastes like manna, and the beer is perfect for washing down your blister-numbing ibuprofen. If your feet call it quits, the hotel offers cheap bunk beds to hold you over until you feel *Braveheart*-good again.

Sleep for Free

While staying at bed-and-breakfasts is an option, it's cheaper (and more fun) to pitch a tent and camp your way through the hike. Per Scottish law, wild camping is allowed except in places where it is posted otherwise, specifically Rannoch Moor, as long as you pick up after your grizzly self and use a civilized camp stove. If indoor plumbing sounds attractive every once in a while, there are designated campsites (with food options nearby) and hostels scattered along the trail, as well.

If you're partial to pristine streams, mossy pine forests, views of Scottish lochs, and glimpses of feral goats and shaggy cows, coupled with giant blisters, missing toenails, and burning muscles, pull up your man-skirt and get trekking.

The Way of the Way

An unspoken mandate of the West Highland Way is to stuff yourself stupid on hearty Scottish food while covering those daily half- (and sometimes full-) marathon distances. One of the iconic landmarks near Loch Lomond is the 300-year-old pub, The Drovers Inn.

This haunted, tumble-down establishment is where cattle drovers stopped for a pint and some haggis as they moved their cattle down from the Highlands for sale and export. Vegetarians wanting to try the local fare can order the neaps and tatties vegetarian haggis, or Scotch broth soup.

The Rowardennan Hotel, another stop along the Way, offers up a meal

WHAT THE F*CK IS HAGGIS?

Hag-story

The first written haggis recipe was found in 1430 in Lancashire in Northwest England, so the nasty train to haggisville has been pulling in and out of the station for a long ass time. Haggis got so popular that in 1787, Robert Burns wrote a poem about it. His "Address to Haggis" points out that true connoisseurs will eat it with "neaps and tatties," turnips or rutabagas and boiled and mashed potatoes. Today, people eat it with whatever they want and wash it down with Scotch, a pint of beer, or whatever alcohol is around to effectively neutralize the taste of sheep insides.

PEOPLE CONSUME SOME pretty nasty shit on planet earth. From black pudding in the U.K. (not chocolaty in the least) to baby mice wine in Korea, the gag factor is sky high. Always up for competition, the Scots throw their hat into the ring with haggis, a delightful national treasure you'll soon learn to puke up with Scottish pride.

What the "Pluck"?

Haggis is made up of sheep's "pluck," or the heart, liver, and lungs of Mary's little lamb. Chefs mash them up with onions, oatmeal, suet, and spices, and moisten the mash with stock before shoving it into the animal's emptied stomach. At which point, it's simmered in stock for about three hours before being dumped onto the plates of hungry, red-faced Scots. As Scotland's national dish, declining an offering of haggis would be unpatriotic.

Hag on This

Scottish restaurants have interpreted haggis in all sorts of ways. In snooty restaurants, try the "Flying Scotsman," a chicken breast hugging a lump of haggis. And since everything is better with bacon, when the "Flying Scotsman" puts on a bacon kilt, you have the dish known as "Chicken Balmoral." Just when you vegetarians thought you were off the hook, since the '60s, vegetarian haggis has been produced with vegetables and various other fillings. Step into a supermarket in Scotland, and you'll have your pick of the haggis litter.

Haggis is as popular as *Braveheart*, and filling your stomach with other stomachs is almost mandatory.

South Africa

GET HIGH, GET LOW, GET SCARED

MOST THRILL-SEEKING BACK-packers first experience Africa by way of South Africa, a country that mashes together some of the best extreme adventures available world-wide. Sure you can Jeep around on a safari, but here are three equally amazing ways to work at least one near-death experience into your trip.

Get High: Table Mountain

Have yourself an adrenaline picnic atop Cape Town's Table Mountain, a landmark you can either admire from the beach, take a cable car to ascend, or (if you're done being a pussy) climb like a rabid beast. Tackle the tougher (adorably named) routes such as Double Jeopardy or Mary Poppins and Her Great Umbrella to prove your prowess. Once your feet are on the mountain's defining plateau (the "table"), peek through the tablecloth of clouds to get tasty views of the Indian and Atlantic oceans, Robben Island (where Mandela was imprisoned), and of all of Cape Town. If your inner junkie hungers for more, have yourself an abseiling adventure and rappel off the side of the mountain. Ropes chaffing your baby-bottom? Diving into Kamikaze Canyon's natural pools should fix you right up.

To nail down unique sleeping arrangements, rev your flaccid calves and take on the Hoerikwaggo Trail from Table Mountain to Cape Point, which includes a stop in the Orange Kloof Forest. While wild camping is forbidden on Table Mountain, you can spend the night in one of the designated camp areas at Orange Kloof Tented Camps on trail starting from the Silvermine Dam. These camps hook you up with everything you need so you can pass out under the Table, safari-style.

Get Low: Surfing South Africa

In South Africa, people don't just

catch waves, they hunt down massive, rolling aqua giants and shred them apart, savoring every bubbling bit. Show off your mad surfing skills by tearing through some of the best waves in the world. For surfing near Cape Town, grab the commuter rail out to Muizenberg, where you can rent wetsuits and boards (and instruction if you need it). Keep your head above water and your ears open for shark sirens.

To get deep into the local surf culture, head to Jeffreys Bay (JBay to the natives), near Port Elizabeth. You won't find too many tourists (unless you go during the Billabong surf festival in July), but you will find enough waves to slap you silly until the sun goes down.

To tackle the biggest breed of wave around, head to Dungeons in Hout Bay. Thirty-foot swells are on the menu at Cape Hout, which is best reached by boat from nearby Cape Town. The Red Bull Big Wave Africa

surf competition takes over some time between early May and mid-August, depending on the waves. Watch the pros wrestle these daemons for inspiration.

Get Scared: Shark Diving Till You Shit Yourself

If the shark tunnel at the local aquarium is the closest you've been to a Great White, get ready to loosen your bowels with the terrifying fun of shark cage diving in the waters of South Africa, where the finned fishies swim. Most expeditions leave from Gansbaai, a fishing village near "Shark Alley." The Alley is a narrow channel between two small islands where sharks love to chomp on the Cape Fur seals that congregate in the area. No need to be dive certified—just make sure you have an intense desire to piss in a wetsuit when a Great White slams up against the cage.

The World's Five Most Challenging Mountains to Climb

THESE PEAKS DON'T CARE IF you have the agility of a rhesus monkey, the sticky toes of a tree frog, or arms like Arnold; they will gloriously ravage you to the core regardless. Checking any one of these mountains off your climbing list will instantly elevate you to the status of climbing royalty.

K2—Border of China and Pakistan (8,612 meters)
Nickname: "The Savage"
Famous for: Second-highest peak in the world; second-highest fatality rate (one out of every four people die trying to reach the summit); has never been climbed in the winter.

KILIMANJARO—Tanzania (5,895 meters)
Nickname: "The Roof of Africa"
Famous for: Highest in Africa; comprised of three volcanoes; not that hard to climb, but a legendary trek.

BAINTHA BRAKK—Pakistan (7,285 meters)
Nickname: "The Ogre"
Famous for: Almost vertical ascent (its South Face rises 3,000 meters across only 2,000 meters); craggy as can be; most bear-infested camp areas.

MOUNT EVEREST—Nepal (8,850 meters)
Nickname: Listen, it's like the Chuck Norris of mountains, so a nickname would be beneath it.
Famous for: Highest mountain peak in the world.

FITZROY—Border of Chile and Argentina, Andes (3,375 meters)
Nickname: "Frigid Fitzgerald"
Famous for: Not a grower or a shower, just icy as fuck, avalanche-prone, and jagged; averages only one ascent per year.

Otp

ART *and* DESIGN

EXPLORE ART OUTSIDE OF THE MUSEUM BOX. GRAFFITI, large-scale murals, sculpture, and creative, multimedia integration is what our generation calls art, and the world is bursting with visual stimulation. Hit New York for a face full of graffiti and Tokyo for head-to-toe tat culture. From the traditional museums of Paris to the makeshift studios of gritty Berlin, the street art culture of New York City to Gaudí's twisted Sagrada Família, the multitude of ways people express themselves around the world will stir you with inspiration, adding depth to your definition of art.

Australia

THE GLUE SOCIETY

A "CREATIVE COLLECTIVE" from Australia, The Glue Society has been sticking it to The Man with the most amazing sculptures, ads, films, and art exhibitions Down Under, over, and everywhere in between. Pop off the cap and take a big whiff of what these sneaky Aussies are cooking.

of both Sydney and New York, and mastering every medium from film to mega-sculpture, this collective is proving that just a dribble of glue is strong enough to hold the entire world's attention.

Glue Who?

In 1998, Jonathon Kneebone and Gary Freedman set out to start an advertising business in Sydney that aimed to transform traditional takes on advertising. With no regard to strategy or media planning, Kneebone and Freedman began creating advertising content that was 100 percent creative—making ads that were way cooler than the shit they were advertising. As the years rolled on and the clients rolled in, this dynamic duo grew into an awesome-gon of eight amazing artists, writers, directors, and designers. Now based out

What the Glue Do

Whether it's a tiny bum taking a shit on top of a giant pigeon's head ("I Heard They're Dirty"), or a massive house raining on the inside ("I Wish You Hadn't Asked"), behind every Society piece lies an idea that is as well thought out as it is executed. "Hot with a Chance of Late Storm" is visual commentary on global warming though a sculpture of a melting ice cream truck in Sydney, and "God's Eye View" uses Jesus and satellite imagery to convey thoughts about naïveté in Miami.

Making It Stick

When Kneebone and Freedman formed their creative alliance, they set out with a simple mission: "to make a living doing what [they] love doing." Not only are the members of the Glue Society still in love with what they're doing, but so is everyone else. Aside from making kickass art, these guys are really good at winning awards, like the prestigious Titanium Lion Award at the Cannes Lions International Festival of Creativity and an award at Denmark's Sculpture by the Sea festival. In a society where you can buy everything from a husband to a hammock online, the Glue Society aims to use technology to highlight what we all need most— simple, human connections.

No longer a secret, this society is taking the art world by storm. If *we* had to create an ad for these guys, it would simply read, "The Glue Society—Australian for *cool-as-fuck*."

Barcelona

GAUDI-LAND

CATALAN TRADITIONALISTS love their fine art museums, and the street kids deck out the cityscape with incredible murals. Local artists are constantly at work, creating mind-bending pieces that build on their artistic history and move it forward. But while many styles and expressions exist in this undoubtedly artsy city, nothing sets Barcelona visually apart from the world more than the architectural contributions of Antoni Gaudí, Barcelona's deranged master of plaster. His drippy, twisted buildings puncture the otherwise classic Spanish city blocks and turn them into stare-worthy attractions.

Solitude Builds Character

All of that quirk definitely came from somewhere. Antoni Gaudí was born in 1852 in Reus and was a sickly kid with rheumatism (creaky joints), which forced him to sit around and look at shit by himself instead of interacting with other kids. Since walking was difficult, Tony rode a donkey and spent his early days observing animals and nature. A vegetarian for most of his life, his respect for nature shone through everything he did. Not surprisingly, he was never much of a people-person and is rumored to have died a seventy-three-year-old virgin.

Learning the Rules to Bend

Gaudí first came to Barcelona in 1868 to study architecture and, even though he was a pretty shitty student, managed to graduate and leave a lasting impression. As is often the case with weirdos, Gaudí's professors thought he was either a complete moron or a total genius. The city of Barcelona took a chance on Gaudí and commissioned him to design lampposts for the Plaça Reial. Although you could blink and miss them, the art nouveau lamps are still lighting the way today. We're betting on genius.

La Familia Sagrada

A Catholic bordering on fanatic, Gaudí dedicated most of his adult life to designing a church that would scare the bejesus out of Jesus. Gaudí began working on La Família Sagrada—the most famous site in Barcelona—in 1882, and it's *still* not finished. The dripping, curling towers hit you in the face as you walk out of the train station, and your eyes take a few minutes to adjust to its insanely unique design. Part Gothic, part Naturalistic, and all Gaudí, La Família Sagrada is so intricate and complex that dozens of architects and builders are still working to realize Gaudí's vision, over 130 years after construction began.

Casa Vicens

With the lampposts, Gaudí gained some serious street cred and was commissioned to build a house for a rich family that owned a ceramic tile factory. From 1883 to 1888, Gaudí worked on Casa Vicens, drawing from his fascination with Oriental details and Moorish architecture to create the ridiculous McMansion. As a tribute to the man who paid him, Gaudí detailed the casa with the owner's multicolor tiles, which made the whole thing look like a shimmering fish at sunrise. His next projects con-tinued to decorate the city with archi-tectural weirdness. Casa Milà, which he completed in 1910, looks like stone waves and was almost too damn weird for the government's approval. Inspired by nature, Gaudí's geometri-cally defying designs can be seen in many other buildings around town, like the Casa Calvet and Casa Batlló. Park Güell is an entire park of surreal-ist sculptures and structures, perching high above the city like a tripped-out thought bubble.

Dali Museum: Figueres

JUST NORTH OF BARCELONA
lies Dali's surrealistic tribute to himself. This theater-turned-museum was curated by the talented media hooker himself and contains important pieces from every stage of Dalí's twisted artistic life. Here, you will find the long-legged elephants, dripping doodles, and funky jewelry that best characterize his style. The Mae West Room, in which art and interior design meld together like the colors in a lava lamp, will bend your mind into submission. Born in Figueres, Dalí made damn sure this museum gave his hometown something to be proud of. The city itself is tiny and has a half-block stretch that resembles La Rambla for ants. Great for day-trip tripping, give Sal a holla when you roll through; his crypt has been chillin' in the center of the museum since 1989.

Death by Trolley

An artist through and through, old man Gaudí was one of those famous guys who dressed like a bum to prove a point. Gaudí was struck by a tram in Barcelona in 1926 and, since he looked less than decent, was given the kind of medical attention homeless people get (i.e., sideways looks and a Band-Aid). When it was discovered that he wasn't a mere (human!) hobo, Gaudí was asked if he wished to be transferred to a better facility, which he declined. After several days in a crappy hospital, Gaudí succumbed to his injuries and died. Point proven. Lesson learned? Listen to your mom and always wear clean underwear because you never know when you'll get hit by a trolley and be mistaken for a homeless person.

Berlin

GRITTY ART, WAREHOUSE SPACES, AND STREET STYLES

BREAKING FREE FROM ITS

Wall-divided days, Berlin is united through its artistic expression. Like the city itself, art in Berlin is innovative, unconventional, and constantly changing with the creative, free spirits of its people who fight control by coloring the machine's monotony. One part raw, one part unrefined, and all parts real, Berlin's explosive art scene will inspire you to get your hands dirty.

Gritty Art

After a lengthy period of historic oppression, the progressively liberal trend that plows forward today is voiced and displayed through the creative artists who live, breathe, and decorate Berlin. Their art tells the tale of a city transcending its past and flourishing in its freedom. As such, themes can cover everything from societal chaos to peace, prosperity, and community. This means that you're as likely to find a portrayal of a decapitated cat's head cooking in an oven as you are a building-size depiction of East and West Berliners uniting. Most will be raunchy; all will be nice.

Warehouse Spaces

The beauty of Berlin is that it's still coming up. A new player in a long-established game, Berlin isn't yet influenced by the poshness and snobbery sometimes associated with art. Exhibits and venues are as down-to-earth as the artists. You'll find dozens of dilapidated buildings inhabited by starving artists showcasing their work all throughout the city, especially in the district of Mitte.

Walk right in and look around; each room has a different flavor, and most of the works are for sale. In Sox, you'll find an all-outdoors gallery on Oranien street in Kreuzberg. Window shopping at its finest, the tiny window space (only a few yards wide) switches up its showcase every few weeks.

Street Styles

Berlin is hailed as the mecca of urban art. First thrown up in the '60s in response to the creation of the Berlin Wall, street art has shifted from cries for equality to mind-fucking murals that turn the city's streets into colorful canvases portraying the political progression. The biggest in the international game—Banksy, Invader, and Blu, to name just a few—have sprayed their marks on Berlin, alongside the works of local guys like El Bocho, Alias, and XOOOOX. Lucky for you, finding street art in Berlin is easy as finding a decent-looking hooker in one of its Red Light districts. For a

sure thing, walk along the East Side Gallery, the largest (just under a mile long), still-standing, segment of the Wall painted by dozens of artists as a freedom memorial.

Currently controlled, inhabited, and decorated by the people, it's no wonder that financial Berlin is dick-deep in debt while artistic Berlin kicks more ass than an underpaid, actually angry dominatrix.

Chile

REPÚBLICA PORTÁTIL

REMEMBER HOW COOL IT
was in fifth grade to sniff glue and
watch your lava lamp morph into different shapes of glowing red blobs?
'Roid that up to mural size, add more
colors and structure, synchronize it
to electronic music, project it onto
street performers, and you have a
production made possible by the
masterminds at República Portátil
(RP). Back in 2002, university students from Concepción, Chile, made
live shows incorporating elements of
the musical arts, visuals, dramatic
architecture, and design. A year later,

the group took to the streets, project-
ing symbolic constructions in vacant
lots. Public space became their canvas—fluid projections that, unlike graffiti, leave no trace and are completely
mobile. Using transmediality, what RP
creates is not an art form in itself but
rather a medium for creating art with
the latest in audiovisual technology,
design, architecture, and whatever
else their clever hearts desire.

Fluydos

A República Portátil original, this
abstract art is projected on outside
building walls, backdrops, and scaf-
folding. The massive projections are
actually initially composed of tiny
drops of dyes, oils, and alcohols, all
mixed in translucent slide compartments and recorded on a micro scale.
The contrasting drops transition the

slide from one abstract art piece to another. The trippy projections are then displayed at a strategically chosen time and on a building or city square to capture an intended audience. The wrong setting would be like Nickelback performing for a college-educated crowd. The projections are complemented by electronic music and can be cast on street performers—making them an integral part of the show, not just a backdrop. RP is constantly evolving with applications in live music and film.

Open Sky Museum

ONCE THE "JEWEL OF THE Pacific," Valparaíso used to be *the* port town for ships rounding the Americas. After the Panama Canal opened, the city traded its bling for a hemp necklace and a paintbrush. These days, Valpo is the unplanned love child of an improvised port town and a Bohemian art city that's home to the Museo a Cielo Abierto (the Open Sky Museum), twenty grand outdoor murals that dot the cobblestone streets in *Cerro Bellavista*. The project was started in the great year of 1969, when local art students painted the empty walls until Chile had its obligatory South American military coup in 1973. When the coup ended in 1990, the murals were revamped with help of big-shot Chilean artists. The original intent of the Open Sky Museum was to give drunks something to look at as they stumblefuck from one bar to another. It is your duty to help the founders realize their dream.

Indonesia

EXTREME SHADOW PUPPETRY

WAYANG KULIT, OR SHADOW puppet theater, is a UNESCO recognized Masterpiece of Oral and Intangible Heritage of Humanity—which is a fancy way of saying that, in Indonesia, playing with puppets is cool as fuck.

Background

The word *wayang*, translated from Javanese, means "shadow," but it generally serves as a blanket term for "theater." Paired with the word *kulit* (which means "skin"), the two together refer to the shadow puppet theater that is a central part of Indonesian culture and heritage. Wayang Kulit is most popular in Java and Bali, although other countries like Sumatra and Lombok like to play with their puppets, too. Since there is no record of Wayang Kulit before Hinduism and the two main performed story lines revolve around the famous Indian epics *The Mahabharata* and *The Ramayana*, it's likely that Wayang Kulit was a gift from Indian traders somewhere around the first century.

The Plot

With few exceptions, all Wayang Kulit performances tell the story of either *The Mahabharata* or *The Ramayana*. Both are epically long (sometimes lasting nine hours) tales of love, evil, good, good prevailing over evil, and how to live life without being a scumbag. The dalang, or puppeteer, must know both these stories as well as his own meat puppet, because he is responsible for voicing every character in the all-night performance. In addition to the traditional plotline, current events, songs, and jokes are thrown in to keep the audience interested (and awake).

The Setting

Wayang Kulit performances are generally commissioned for special events like religious holidays, weddings, cremations, and rite-of-passage ceremonies. Since it's an all-night affair with food and festivities, Wayang Kulit is something to get excited about—like how you'd get excited about a Guns N' Roses concert.

Casting the Shadow

Although they are in shadows during the performance, the construction and detail of each Wayang Kulit puppet is a work of art unto itself. Putting a puppet together takes a team of artists a few weeks to finish. Like a runway model, a top-notch puppet begins

will speak for the people and address the issues that are most important to them. Under traditional law, the dalang is not considered responsible for anything he says during a performance—giving him artistic license to talk shit freely.

Showtime!

Once the sun goes down and the white, cloth screen goes up, the dalang assembles his cast "backstage." The good-guy characters are arranged on the right-hand side of the stage and the bad-guys on the left—with the center area used as the stage. The orchestra (*gamelan*) sits at their respective instruments and waits for the head homeboy, the dalang, to signal the start with a tap of his foot. Once the oil lamp is lit and the shadows are cast, the dalang lubes up his fingers and voice, and then begins the show!

with good skin (from a buffalo), which is then smoothed, primed, intricately chiseled, and painted before it's ready to make a stage debut.

Putting the Dang! in Dalang

Like in *The Wizard of Oz*, you'll want to pay close attention to the man behind the curtain. Part puppeteer extraordinaire, part conductor via foot-tapping, social commentator, artist, and all-around funny guy, the dalang is to Wayang Kulit what a president is to a democratic nation (minus the lies). The *dalang* is considered a sacred artist in Indonesia and is highly revered. Aside from controlling a whole cast of puppets and bringing each of them to life vocally, the dalang is also responsible for incorporating local flava into his story line. Using two clown-like characters (*panakawan*) in the cast, the dalang

How the Indonesians Stay Awake

TASTES LIKE COFFEE

Finding a supplier to meet your caffeine demand shouldn't be hard in a region sited as the fourth-largest producer of coffee in the world. Dutch colonists first introduced coffee to Jakarta in 1696, and thanks to a perfect climate, the plant grew into a major cash crop by 1725. Although Indonesians drink less than half of the almost 500,000 metric tons of coffee produced in their region, they still manage to suck down a good portion of the brown stuff.

TASTES LIKE CANCER

Move over Red Bullshit—*Extra Joss* and *Kuku Bima* have you beat on any Indonesian street. Just add a packet of either of these powdered mysteries to a glass of water and watch your energy grow! Active ingredients in both include royal jelly, ginseng, taurine, caffeine, and B-vitamins. If you're planning to watch a man play with a puppet for nine hours, these crackity mixes are excellent discreet pick-you-ups.

New York City

THE GRANDADDY OF GRAFFITI

WHERE IT ALL BEGAN, THE street art in New York City still decorates all of its extremities—from roofs to bodegas to subway tunnels—creeping into tourist photos, and dazzling up advertisements and bar bathrooms. Lace your kicks, look out for the cops, and shake up your paint can—we're throwing up our tag on the NYC graffiti game.

The Birth of Tagging

The NYC street art craze began in the late 1960s when a teenage foot-messenger known best as Taki 183 started to spray his name all across northern Manhattan. Although it's said that another graffiti writer, Julio 204, brought tagging to Manhattan, Taki 183's fame—including a 1971 *New York Times* cover story—is credited for inspiring others to test their hand at painting up the city's streets.

While some were "getting up" slowly, others "bombed" 'hoods to get their names out there quickly, outfitting Lower East Side tenement buildings in top-to-bottom tags. Bombing hit its heyday in the early '70s and remains popular today.

Moving art installations were created when artists took their talents to the subways. With competition for recognition rising, artists worked at

night alongside rats while tagging subway cars to move their names throughout the boroughs. Subway cars were wrapped in murals, a large-scale design pioneered by the artist known as Super Kool 223 and mastered by the infamous graffiti quintet, The Fabulous Five.

Just as shit got really interesting, the *Clean Train Movement of 1989* decommissioned any train with graffiti on it—leading to poor enough service that the graffiti masters eventually stopped. The MTA is only now realizing how much it pissed off its art-appreciating riders and recently launched various public art promotions—or PG attempts at "cleaning up" graffiti by replacing it with city-approved art. Luckily, regardless of its legality, underground street artists continue to thrive aboveground. Street art in New York continues to grow, spanning vertical space from high up on rooftops, to the ground level and down into mole-people territory.

Artists You Should Know

Known for either pioneering a certain style, collaborating on murals, or just covering a lot of city space, in NYC, these artists are essential to the scene:

TRACY 168

Known for creating Wildstyle graffiti by fusing block, bubble, and curling lettering styles.

FAB 5 FREDDY

Notorious for merging the hip-hop nation with the graffiti underworld of New York. Although it has long been said that graffiti is simply a visual representation of hip-hop, according to Freddy, both are separate artistic forms of counterculture. ▼

DR. REVOLT

Another old-school artist, the "doctor" painted up subways cars with the best of them. His mainstream claim to fame was designing the logo for *Yo! MTV Raps*. Word to your mother.

◀

CORTES ▲

Best recognized for his Metallica-esque skulls and sharp, angular lettering, Cortes continues to impress spectators at 5 Pointz with new pieces and a recent collaboration with Meres, another popular NYC graffiti artist.

COPE2 ▲

From the South Bronx, Fernando Carlo has been at it since the late '70s, and you can find his bubbled-out name just about anywhere from SoHo billboards to video games to chucks. From time to time, Banksy pops into the city to stencil up building sides or sneak his dark humor into museum installations.

OTP TIP: For great videos documenting tons of NYC graffiti in progress (with a bit of Kim Kardashian's booty), check out Mrdutch730.

TATS CRU ▲
(AKA THE MURAL KINGS)

Tats Cru are muralists (the original three were from the Bronx) who have been painting up large NYC walls and subways for twenty-five years. Artists continue to join the crew every year, painting larger and more elaborate murals, competing in graffiti battles, and even taking part in a documentary to promote their craft. A famous member of the "Cru" was Fat Joe, whose tag name was "Crack."

Finding Street Art

From personal to political, various meaningful pieces cover the city from sewers to delis to bridges to your hostel to our house and back. You're bound to find at least simple tags on any given street block or subway station, and with graffiti becoming more mainstream, advertisers are commissioning artists to create intricate murals for their campaigns. Should you feel like getting in the thick of it, check out:

5 POINTZ

On the ground level, when it comes to sheer abundance, Queens is the king of New York graffiti. The 5 Pointz studio in Long Island City is a living graffiti collage, where international artists produce attention-grabbing pieces on and in this abandoned warehouse.

THE GRAFFITI HALL OF FAME

Wrapping an old playground on 106th and Park in East Harlem, this wall has been in a state of artistic evolution for three decades. Home to live graffiti battles, the biggest names in New York street art venture to this famed concrete slab to throw up their pieces.

THE LOWER EAST SIDE

Housing a large concentration of skinny, starving artists, this part of the city contains the legendary graffiti wall near the intersection of Houston and Bowery that has displayed the stylings of various artists for over thirty years. While it's now a fully legal spot to spray, the art that graces its facade changes frequently and is still pretty impressive. Also, you'll be glad to know that the historical tenement buildings are still tagged to shit.

Train Windows

THE BEST GRAFFITI WINDOW-WATCHING CAN BE DONE FROM the G train as it emerges above-ground over 5 Pointz from Brooklyn to Queens (stops: between 21 St.-Jackson Avenue and Court Square).

London

THE STREETS ARE ALIVE WITH THE SOUND OF SPRAY CANS

NEXT TO BEING A DRUNK, pikey football fan, graffiti is up high there on the list of ways to piss off a bobby in London. Government officials there have launched a massive crackdown to ensure the streets and tube trains are visually clean, but street artists are still slathering the town with colorful images and antiestablishment messages. Take a trip down tagging lane with our rough sketch of the street artists lurking in London.

BANKSY ▲

A household name that even your mom might recognize, Banksy pushed stenciling to the forefront of street art. Using an escapist technique, in which a stencil is made beforehand and then used to spray quickly on-site, Banksy has received a lot of praise (and shit) for his sarcastic displays of discontent with society. While his work is all over the world (in some of the most controversial places), he pops up every now and again in his homeland. His satirical style and semi-secret identity keep him in the street-art spotlight.

KING ROBBO ▲

The feud between King Robbo and Banksy runs deep, and neither seems willing to acquiesce. In 1985, Robbo painted a huge, full-color piece called "Robbo Incorporated" next to Regent's Canal in Camden. The area was only accessible by water, but people managed to cover it with graffiti anyway. In 2009, some suspiciously Banksy-esque stencil art turned up, covering most of Robbo's work with the images of a workman pasting wallpaper. That same year, on Christmas (the nerve!), Robbo made it look like the workman was painting "King Robbo" in silver letters. Like a bad tennis match, a few days later, the letters "Fuc" turned up before "King." The two continued to hassle one another, instigating a rather notable graffiti war. It wasn't until 2011, when Robbo suffered a life-threatening head injury, that Banksy let it go . . . sort of.

In an homage effort, Banksy created a piece that supported Robbo's style, but also included his own commentary with a candle lit to resemble a "no fire" emblem. A street-art white flag? We'll see.

OZMO ▶

Ozmo is an Italian tagger who put his mark on London's facade with his "Big Fish Eat Small Fish" slogan down near Shoreditch High Street. Ozmo took the idea from an old Pieter Bruegel the Elder painting and mixed it with an Ingres's painting, *The Turkish Bath*. Inspired by all he finds seedy with London, Ozmo's art focuses on the idea that people only care about money, business, and fame.

MILO TCHAIS

Brazilian street artist Tchais moved to London in 2001 to get his piece of the graffiti pie. His works emphasize shapes, color contrasts, and textures, all through an abstract eye. Like a Picasso/Van Gogh merger, Tchais loves relating his tagging to nature, bringing a softer, more fine-arts approach to street doodles.
◀

EVOL

Berlin-based EVOL moved into Smithfield Market, in central London, to create a miniature city. Using paste-ups and stencils, EVOL turns urban items like concrete blocks, tree planters, and telephone booths into mini-towers. Together, the clusters look like tiny city streets and are a total mind-fuck to look at as London bustles about.

COMMER
WASTE SERVICE
Tel: 020 7364 3364

Paris

THE WHOLE ART EXPERIENCE

PARIS IS REALLY JUST ONE big fucking art exhibit. From the world's most trafficked museum to an oil stain on the sidewalk, Parisians have managed to put art everywhere and make everything art. Suffer through the long gallery lines, discover some hidden gems, and soak up the massive street art scene to get the complete art experience.

Musée du Louvre

WHY OTHERS GO

A G at best, the "beautiful" *Mona Lisa* is somehow the most famous painting in the world. It has also been declared the most overrated tourist attraction in Europe. When you fight through a sea of old people to view the 30 x 21–inch painting behind a barricade and bulletproof glass, you'll understand why.

WHY YOU SHOULD GO

Luckily, the Louvre redeems itself with 35,000 other pieces that solidify its spot as the best collection in the world. Also, there's enough naked-ness here to fill the coffee table book *Le Louvre Nu* ("The Nude Louvre"), which stars the museum's most beautiful women. Mona Lisa isn't among them.

THEN HIT THE STREETS

Paris's Belleville neighborhood is the Louvre of street art. Works from every major French street artist is here—including Blek le Rat, JR, Fred le Chevalier, Kouka, Invader, and the 1984 crew. The street art clusterfuck down Rue Dénoyez is the climax, and like any good orgy, it rotates its contributors often.

The Centre Pompidou
WHY OTHERS GO

Pompidou's National Museum of Modern Art is the second largest collection of modern and contemporary art in the world, with work from Kandinsky, Picasso, Dalí, and Andy Warhol. Its BPI public library is a favorite among local college students. Like Paris's other art museums, the entrance lines routinely spill onto the street.

WHY YOU SHOULD GO

If you want to avoid the crowd or need to save that eight-euro entrance fee for crepes, check out the free Atelier Brancusi modern art museum on Pompidou's plaza. Constantin Brancusi was a Romanian sculptor who spent most of his life in Paris. In his will, he left the entire contents of his small Montparnasse studio—from column sculptures to chisels—to the French state on the condition that the studio would be reconstructed exactly as it was the day he died. The museum is a glimpse into the creation of his abstract work and his obsession with the spatial relationship of his pieces.

THEN HIT THE STREETS

Even more discreet than the Atelier Brancusi, the subjects of Sandrine Boulet's work are everyday street sites that wouldn't normally catch your attention. Boulet photographs regular objects, then adds illustrations to transform them. An ironing board becomes a butterfly, an excavator becomes a giraffe, an oil stain becomes the hair of Amy Winehouse, and a debris chute and bush become the lower half of a well-endowed Adam and an au naturale Eve. Why Boulet messes with street scenery? Her words: "When you are a kid, you spend hours laying down in the grass seeing/visualizing amazing things in the clouds. Well, I have decided this should never stop."

Musée d'Orsay
WHY OTHERS GO

In the birthplace of impressionism, Orsay bridges the art movement gap between the Louvre and Pompidou. Plenty of works by Monet, Manet, Renoir, Degas, and Van Gogh make it worth the stop, but with three million visitors a year, the elbow room gets a little tight.

WHY YOU SHOULD GO

The setting, a majestic nineteenth-century train terminal, was almost demolished before being converted into a museum. While tourists funnel through the permanent exhibits, the ever-evolving and always impressive temporary exhibits get much less attention. Orsay also hosts lunchtime concerts, film screenings, and festivals for when you need a little more free movement.

THEN HIT THE STREETS

Princess Hijab, Paris's most reclusive street artist, exhibits her work in train stations in much shorter-term, temporary exhibits. Late at night, Hijab paints black veils over the faces and airbrushed half-naked bodies of subway fashion advertisements. Her motives could be to draw attention to France's Islamophobic laws against Muslim headdresses or to combat in-your-face sexuality. No one knows who she is, and it's unclear if she really is Muslim or even a female.

Rome

ETERNAL GODS OF THE ARTS

FOR 2,500 YEARS, "THE

Eternal City" has been pumping out masterpieces in stone and on canvas. From its distinctive ancient architecture during Rome's golden age to the defining sculptures and paintings of the Renaissance, Rome has somehow managed to preserve its art history through centuries of war, earthquakes, and neglect. These are the still-standing highlights from Rome's two greatest eras in this giant museum of a city with a killer food court.

Way Back in the Day: Ancient Rome

In 500 B.C., Rome laid the first bricks of the Forum, which served as the headquarters for all things Roman as it spent the next millennium rising to and falling from the top of the Western world. The Coliseum is the greatest standing work of Roman architecture and engineering. Back in the day, this is where gladiators slaughtered each other to the delight of the Roman public. The Pantheon is the best-preserved ancient Roman building and was used continuously throughout history as a gathering place for the army, then Catholics, then dead people, and now tourists.

When Things Got Real Artsy: Renaissance

The Renaissance, which means "rebirth," marks the period in the fifteenth century when Rome woke up from its 1,000-year-long power nap (otherwise known as the Middle Ages) and decided to regain its awesomeness. Romans rediscovered the works of their golden age, which inspired new movements in literature, science, politics, and most importantly, art. The ceiling of the Sistine Chapel is the masterpiece of all things Renaissance and resides with the pope, in the Vatican City.

In slight violation of the Catholic church's poverty vow, the Vatican Museums and St. Peter's Basilica hold an art collection worth hundreds of billions of dollars. That popular chapel ceiling, Michelangelo's most famous work, is amongst the holdings, although he only reluctantly agreed to Pope Julius II's insistence that he create it. In the pope's defense, there is no better way to say "I love Jesus" than intimidating an artist into spending four years painting 5,000-square-feet of ceiling teetering a deadly sixty-five feet in the air. Other infamous works here include Raphael's *The School of Athens*, Michaelangelo's *Pietà*, Ignazio Danti's *Gallery of Maps*, and Leonardo's *St. Jerome in the Wilderness*.

Still Old, Newer Art: Post Renaissance

It would have been easy for Rome to call it quits after the Renaissance, sit back with a cannoli, and just marvel at its work, but that wouldn't be very "eternal." A walk around the city will lead you to plenty of more recent gems. The Spanish Steps are great for chilling or working off that gelato. If you throw a coin in the Trevi Fountain, you're guaranteed to return to Rome. Since there's no way you'll tackle all of Rome in one visit (it took the rest of Europe four centuries), those twenty euro cents may be a smart investment.

Where in the World is Jesus?

PEOPLE AROUND THE WORLD LOVE THEM A GOOD, OLD-FASHIONED Jesus sculpture, the taller the better. Chances are, wherever you may find yourself, Jesus is hovering somewhere nearby. This is our Jesus dream team.

1. **CHRIST THE KING**—Sylwester Zawadzk, from Świebodzin Poland, was one sneaky priest. He threw a crown on top of JC-Dilla to make him (technically) the tallest Jesus statue in the world.

2. **CRISTO DE CONCORDIA**—This Jesus statue in Cochabamba, Bolivia, would like to remind that poser in Poland that without the crown, Concordia's Cristo reigns supreme.

3. **CHRIST BLESSING**—The "first flying tallest statue in the world" has JC lookin' like he might blow away in Manado City, Indonesia.

4. **CHRIST THE REDEEMER**—Built from 1922–31, this Jesus in Rio de Janeiro, Brazil, may not be the biggest, or the shiniest, but he's definitely been in more movies than all the others combined.

5. **KING OF KINGS (AKA "TOUCHDOWN JESUS")**—Not even Jesus could save this sixty-two-foot sculpture of his bust in Monroe, Ohio, from being struck by lightning and destroyed by fire in 2010.

Tokyo

TATTOO CULTURE

WHILE THE SPARTANS WERE busy manhandling Xerxes in 300 B.C., the Japanese were inking up. Even before ink, the indigenous Ainu of Japan were marking and scarring themselves with tribal designs to represent honor and beauty. When the Meijis outlawed tattooing in 1868, it was driven underground, and like anything illegal, the more illicit tattooing got, the cooler it became. Nowadays, tattoos are a sacred art form that still make a rebel statement, and there are more than 500 parlors across Japan.

Needles All Over

Think that back-piece makes you hard? Traditional *irezumi* covers the entire body, shoulder to foot, front to back, with one un-inked strip down the middle in the front. A person apprentices for years to be a master tattooer of the traditional *irezumi* style, and his teacher even gives him a special name: Hori (carved) + the adopted name of the teacher. The most famous shop in Japan, Scratch Addiction in Tokyo, was the country's first official parlor and is still a pilgrimage site for all serious irezumi enthusiasts. Unique to Japan, this style of tats is only for those serious about pain.

Can't Make a Full-Body Commitment?

The country that gave the world Pokémon and Princess Mononoke has been around the artist block. Men used to hold a monopoly of using or going under the gun, but modern Japanese ladies love their ink. Several top artists in Japan are women, and lady-run Studio Muscat in Tokyo is your best bet for a black and gray. If you're going for color, a dragon symbolizing good luck and wealth is a popular Japanese tattoo. Another good one is a half-sleeve cherry blossom, a Samurai shout-out to honor life's pleasures. If you're an anime nerd looking to represent, hook up with a master geek at Chopstick Tattoo in Osaka.

Look but Don't Prick

The Yokohama Tattoo Museum, run by Horiyoshi III (Japan's unofficial Tattoo King), is a must for any fan of ink culture. It's a small museum dedicated to his personal collection of weird-ass things like shrunken heads. Since a tat at the studio upstairs costs as much as a Prius, give this place a long hard look and take your needle-cravings to the many other shops in the area.

FASHION

WE MAY BE FILTHY, BUT DAMN IT, WE'VE STILL GOT STYLE.
Every city around the world has its own fashionable flair, and while the high-end stuff won't squeeze into your budget (or look good crumpled in your backpack), there are thrifty ways to stay on top of the fashion pulse no matter where you find yourself. Whether you're sporting the candy colors of Stockholm, secondhand store-hopping in NYC, or haggling down the price of leather overalls in Italy, all you need to look good abroad is a little creativity and confidence (and perhaps a hot shower).

HK IN HK:
HELLO KITTY FASHIONS

WITH OVER 20,000 OFFICIAL
HK products on the market, and
Hello Kitty-themed-fucking everything, this cat has her claws deep into
the hearts (and pockets) of all of Asia,
especially Hong Kong—where she
has held office as the Official Ambas-
sador of Tourism since 2008.

Kitty CULTure

Born in Japan, Kitty White—street
name: Hello Kitty—said *konnichiwa* for
the first time in 1974. Sometime before
Miss White's feline face hawked its first
product (a coin purse), the Japanese
began adopting the *kawaii* ("cute" or
"adorable") culture—spawning a phenomenon of happy-good-fun-lucky
times on everything from keychains to
couture. The Japanese company Sanrio hopped on the cute-train when
Yuko Shimizu, an in-house designer,
drew a white, Japanese bobtail cat
with a big red bow and no mouth.

Sanrio wanted to keep their signature
kitty mute so that people "could project their (own) feelings onto the character." Our feeling is that this cat will
give it up to anyone (Nike, Vans,
Kimmora Lee Simmons, Swarovski,
Stüssy, Fender) who's willing to pay to
play with her.

Big Kitty Styles

While fashion trends come and go, in
Hong Kong the kitty is always in style.
On the streets, you will find a colorful
array of feline fashions. HK's face is
printed on absolutely everything:
shoes, shirts, bags, and coats, often
in loud and clashing combined outfits
dedicated to nothing but cat. Raining
out? Grab your trusty HK umbrella to
keep your HK raincoat dry. What time
is it? According to your HK wrist-
watch, it's always Hello Kitty o'clock.

Good Kitty

What is it about this pasty cat with a
big-ass head that people go meowz-
ers over? The ultimate example of
"right time, right place," people asked
for cute—Sanrio gave them a cat
without a mouth. And although she
may not say much, this doesn't seem
to stop freakish followers from buying just about anything with Hello
Kitty's face on it. Stop by the Hello
Kitty store in Hong Kong and pick up
your very own Hello Kitty ice cream
churner, humidifier, bedazzled
hoodie, or hot dog maker! And next
time you think about tying the knot,
consider booking the Hong Kong
subway station and riding the "Hello
Kitty Wedding Train" like one couple

did in 2007—the bride was dazzling in her Hello Kitty wedding dress, which matched her Hello Kitty engagement ring *purr*fectly.

Bad Kitty

If the 20,000 official Hello Kitty products aren't enough, perhaps you could browse through the millions of *un*official products, like the Hello Kitty ball-gag or Hello Kitty latex bed. Pick up a bottle of Hello Kitty Pink Grey Goose Vodka or a sixer of Hello Kitty Beck's. And nothing screams *kawaii*, peace, and love, like the custom Hello Kitty AK-47.

Even though this kitty has no mouth, we're convinced she is laughing all the way to the bank. With a stronghold on the street fashions of Hong Kong, Ms. Kitty is reaping over $5 billion each year, and there's no sign that anyone will sour of this old puss anytime soon.

Pussy Pilot

TAIWANESE EVA AIR CAN fly you into Hong Kong in proper Hello Kitty style. Each plane in their limited Asian route is decorated in one of five themes: Hello Kitty Happy Music Time, Hello Kitty Loves Apples, Hello Kitty with Magic Stars, Hello Kitty Around the World, and Hello Kitty Speed Puff. From the giant pink HK kiosks to a silhouette of the feline's face on every food item served on-board (kitty cantaloupe, anyone?)—every detail is the cat's meow.

Italy

COUNTERFEIT IT: A GUIDE TO KNOCKOFF SHOPPING IN ITALY

IT'S ESTIMATED THAT TEN percent of all designer goods in Italy are big ol' fakers. The demand for Pucci, Gucci, and other high-end Italian brands that don't end in "ucci" are as fierce as the price tags of these coveted items. Don't be fooled by the seemingly fancy getups of high-strutting Italians; knockoffs can be bought everywhere, and even though no Italian would admit to wearing fake Prada, check the tag next time you get a local to drop their pants.

Paying the Price

Before you start hagglin' for a fake Fendi backpack to fill with knockoff goods that are "Made in Italy," consider the pricey consequences for buying counterfeits: a fine of up to 10,000 euros. In an attempt to drastically reduce the demand for rip-off label whoring, the Italian authorities are holding the shopper accountable—even the "unsuspecting" tourist, unaware of law, could end up coughing up 1,000 euros for Prada's pleather cousin.

Goodies On-the-Go

If you are willing to risk the fines for a fake, you don't have to look very hard or spend an Armani-and-a-leg to find one. When in Rome, head toward the area near the Spanish Steps—the equivalent of New York's Fifth Avenue or Paris' Champs-Élysées—to gawk at the OG's, then look for the guys peddlin' on the pavement with big, black duffel bags for more affordable options. In need of some free afternoon entertainment? Hang around and wait for the *polizia* to roll through—the makeshift shops for fakes turn mobile in an instant as the "shop owners" flee the authorities. Florence and Milan host the same scene. Look for a crowd of tourists surrounding goods on the ground, then look right and left for coppers before buying.

Label-less Leathers

If you can give a shit less about labels, then your options for bagging quality Italian goods—like leather—without risking run-ins with the law significantly increase. Bring home a real souvenir made of Italian leather by sifting through the skins in Florence, the leather capital of Italy. The Santa Croce Leather Workshop, located in the cloister of the Santa Croce church, is the leathery Mecca, but also take a look-see at the San Lorenzo Market, where bringing your bargaining game face is essential. Wandering off the beaten path of any market can host perfect "leather-weather"—head down the side streets of smaller villages for a personal experience with artisans and a chance to score more for less.

Whether riskin' a bad rap for a good price or ditching the label and paying less, there is no shortage of deals to be found on Italy's fashionable streets. No matter what the label on your bag says, it should never read: full price.

VENDORS EVERYWHERE ARE LIKE HUNGRY HAWKS, AND A

shopping tourist is their wounded prey. They'll be watching you from the moment you enter the market, sniffing for weakness. So, put on your best scowl, get focused, and stay sharp. Keep these tips tucked in your pocket to score big discounts on random shit at the market:

1. Know how much you are willing to spend before entering the playing field, and don't be afraid to walk away.

2. Face it: no one's buying that you're a local, but knowing a few key phrases in the local language will open the cheap shopping floodgates.

3. Haggling is like dating. You have to romance the vendor a little before you get the goods. However, unlike dating, no never means no in this deceptive relationship. Wink, smile, and nod as you talk up his treasure, then "psshhh!" at what he says it costs. Once he's drunk off your haggling charm, take it all the way home!

4. Know that his starting price is always at least twice as much as he's willing to sell an item for, and level the playing field by offering half of what you're down to pay.

5. A skilled vendor will tug at your heartstrings or fuck with your head to gain access to your wallet. Stick to your plan regardless of whether his fifteen daughters need braces. Even if your new vendor buddy puts his arm around your shoulder, serves you tea, and tells you stories he's never told anyone, you don't owe him shit.

6. If you find yourself agreeing with him when you initially didn't, take a step away for some fresh air. Chances are whatever you want will still be there once you return, this time with ice running through your veins.

7. When it comes to haggling, sometimes lying is the best policy. "The guy down the block o'er there has this same exact thing for three bucks cheaper. Should I just go buy it from him?"

8. Buying in bulk adds leverage. If you have extra room in your pack, the two-for-one haggling trick can get you what you want, plus another something you may not want.

Once you're both winded from the bargaining boogie, the final step is to look the vendor straight in the eye, lay down your final offer, and shut the fuck up. Let it linger like a silent-but-deadly fart. Stand there and bask in the stench, until he either gives in to your offer, or you cave and buy the damn elephant statue for thirty cents more.

OTP TIP: Offer the vendor half the asking price *minus one*. Since half is the expected counter-wager, going one lower shows that you know the game and mean business. He'll either be impressed by your showmanship or think you're a jerk-off.

New York City

SECONDHAND CLOTHES THAT DON'T SMELL LIKE MOTHBALLS

FASHION RULES NEW YORK.
The streets are like runways with style oozing from every corner. What's that? You didn't pack the new Dolce & Gabbana spring line into your backpack? Fear not. Although famous Fifth Avenue is lined with stores even your sugardaddy (or mama) couldn't afford, there are several low-budget options when it comes to shopping for threads. As important as fashion is here, creativity takes precedence (and that's free). So use the streets for inspiration and find creative, cheaper alternatives at the places below.

Buffalo Exchange and Beacon's Closet

These are two chains that work in similar ways. Both are combo stores of both new and secondhand clothes and accessories, with several stores in Brooklyn and Manhattan. The stores are well organized and have sections for both girls and guys. The merchandise in this store works in a wonderful way. Basically, sellers bring in their gently used, recently fashionable clothes, then a skilled clerk sorts through their stuff and picks items

they feel will sell best. The seller can then choose to either get store credit or cash for the items the store takes.

What this all means to you, especially in New York, is that you get to scavenge through nice, almost new, fashionable things and pay very little for your finds. Additionally, the items you find reflect the neighborhood in which they're sold, so you really get a sense of the local fashion preferences.

Century 21

A retailer of discounted designer clothing, shoes, and accessories, their motto is "fashion worth fighting for." If buying big name brands without the high price tags is your thing, this is the place to go. The styles are often for older people, but you can find a good deal if you look hard. This place is huge, so you will get your fashion fight on—for hours.

Goodwill/ Salvation Army

There is nothing shameful about shopping at Goodwill. Whereas people used to equate these stores with soup kitchens, the plummet of the American economy has brought new interest to these places. Sure these stores are full of some pretty useless junk, but lots of fashionable New Yorkers donate their sassy stuff to these places for tax write-offs, so it may be worth the dig.

The trick to keeping up with New York style on a budget is steering away from the conventional and shopping at places that require a little more browsing. After all, in this fashionable city, one man's trash is probably much more fashionable than your own trash.

Peru

DRESSED TO KILL

IF YOU THOUGHT LOVEABLE little guinea pigs couldn't get any cuter, the town of Huacho, Peru, has taken their preciousness to a new level. In the annual Festival of the Guinea Pig, our snugalicious pets are dressed in darling outfits to look like furry, pint-size people and compete for the titles of absofuckinglute adorability. Over in the food stalls however, some of their less fortunate colleagues are fried whole and served with rice and veggies. Guinea pigs star in every part of the festival—from the main stage to the main course.

Before You Judge . . .

Long before Mr. Fluff Monster was your kindergarten classroom pet, guinea pigs were domesticated by the Andean people for their meat, not their cuddliness. Called *cuy* (pronounced "kwee") in Spanish and rarely, but more accurately, *cavy* (pronounced "KAY-vee") in English, they bang like bunnies and taste (almost) like chicken. These cheap, low-maintenance rodents grow up fast and are lean in fat and high in protein. In rural Andean homes, you'll

find dozens of cuy frolicking and fornicating at will—until someone gets hungry. They are not pets, nor pigs, nor from Guinea . . . so we pretty much got it completely wrong.

The Fashion Show

Villages throughout Ecuador, Peru, and Bolivia throw annual fiestas to honor these rats with better PR. In Huacho, the cuy catwalk takes center stage. Many are dressed in traditional outfits, often to match their owners. Others are dressed as kings, nobles, farmers, peasants, miners, folk singers, and even Santa Claus. Prizes are dished out for the best-dressed cuy, along with the fattest, fastest, and of course, tastiest. You won't find an official website about this July festival, so brush up your Español, fly down to Lima, catch a bus up the coast to Huacho, and ask around. Pack a tiny trumpet and bow tie for Cuy Armstrong, a mini coonskin cap for Cavy Crockett, and some hair grease and a secondhand suit for My Cousin Guinea. You could be the first gringo winner, or even participant, the festival has ever seen. And you probably already know what's served at the victory dinner.

Stockholm

WHAT'S UNDER THAT PARKA?

YOU MIGHT THINK OF PARIS, Milan, or Tokyo as cities on the cutting edge of style—but the land that birthed Ikea and H&M brings big Nordic fashion cojones to the table, as well. Many of the styles you're sporting this year have been in full trendy swing in Sweden since before you knew what a fedora was. Stockholm is all about accessible fashions, and even though it gets ass-cold over there, they still manage to have loads of style peeking out from under their parkas.

Squeeze into the Rainbow

Skinny jeans are a fairly recent trend in the States but have been around Stockholm for years. Never mind boring blue denim, these guys blow it out with skittles-bright colors like Fanta-orange, John Deere-green and cherry pie-red. Pair with a collared shirt and cardigan carelessly tossed over the shoulders, and you'll seamlessly integrate into the rainbow of pedestrians on the streets of Stockholm.

Men in Pink

Colorful clothing in Stockholm knows no gender boundaries. The guys have shed their masculine Viking ancestry and don't mind sporting lavender suits (cut skinny and short is the standard), bubble gum–pink shirts, and magenta scarves. Swedes believe in healthcare and color for all.

OTP TIP: Don't freak out if you pop into a Cheap Monday or an Acne (unfortunate name, kick-ass clothing store) and can't find clothes segregated by sex. Swedes are into unisex clothing styles and don't discriminate based on hotdogs or hallways.

Over-the-Shoulder Boulder Holder

Scarves are wardrobe staples in this frigid land. Most are wrapped front to back (start with the scarf at your throat, take the ends to your back, and wrap it to the front again with the ends dangling down) and are meant to add a pop of color to boring black coats. In Stockholm, thicker

is better with scarves and sausages—don't get caught with a thin and puny one in the freezing winter.

Big Woodies

Sweden didn't invent the clog, but it's been a fashion staple since ABBA exported the look around the world in the '70s. In 2007, the clog reemerged in Stockholm fashion when Cilla Wingård Neuman and Emy Blixt started "Swedish Hasbeens," their line of updated clogs, upon discovering hundreds of vintage pairs in the basement of a factory near Stockholm.

SERIOUS FASHION

LIKE THE REGION ITSELF, West African fashion is often misrepresented. Stereotyped as a place that is too poor to care about fashion or too exotic to be relevant, West Africa doesn't just offer animal print threads and crazy tribal neck gear. On the contrary, the region is pumping out some serious fashion that's quickly creepin' onto every major, modern runway from New York to Milan.

Fabric of West African Fashion

Traditional textiles, as bold and original as the West African people and their history, are setting trends on every continent. Those sweet, colorful, geometric leggings you scored at Urban Outfitters—they were probably inspired by Ghanaian *kente* cloth. When the Akan people of Ghana and the Ivory Coast first introduced the most famous of all African fabrics, it was considered a fabric fit only for a king.

Nowadays, kente-style cloth is fitting just about every class of hot ass around the globe. Those boldly patterned, batik-style fabrics that are being turned into designer booty-shorts for Beyoncé or a one-of-a-kind jacket for Lady Gaga—every designer from Marc Jacobs to Tory Burch can thank West African Ankara fabric for influencing their designs. And although the *Ankara*-style was a result of Dutch-colonial influence, West Africans immediately spun their creativity and cultural heritage into every fiber of the signature cloth.

Striking a Pose

Unlike many of the Western fashion trends that are dictated by massive marketing campaigns, West African fashion celebrates creativity, originality, and the importance of personal style. Many West Africans choose to entertain their inner Armani by picking a fabric they connect with and commissioning a seamstress to make the

garment just the way they want. Talented designers are emerging from this scene, like Nigerian Lisa Folawiyo, founder of world-renowned brand *Jewel by Lisa*. Her ever-evolving lines celebrate the deep cultural and social significance of traditional fabrics in their designs—with an added personal touch, like Swarovski crystal embroidering. Judging by the hordes of Western world copycats, West Africa has become a big fucking fashion deal.

Name-Droppin'

Maybe Deola Sagoe is not a household name like Coco Chanel, but this Nigerian designer has peeps like Oprah and Will Smith begging for her haute couture. Expect to hear more about 2012 *Arise* Magazine Fashion Week Emerging Artist of the Year recipient, Loza Maléombho. Raised in Ivory Coast and based out of NYC, this edgy designer is using fashion not only to raise awareness of the West African heritage, but also as a tool for the social empowerment of West African women. She employs local women from Ivory Coast, pays them fair wages, teaches them how to manage money, and showcases their talents on the global runway. Although the region is still shrouded in images of *National Geographic* loin cloths, West Africa is combining its dynamic history and modern artistry to produce unique, street-ready fashion.

Making Cash Out of Trash

MAKING USE OF IMPORTED WESTERN GARBAGE, LIKE PLASTIC

and glass bottles, West Africans have found numerous ways to turn junk into jingles. Ghana takes bead lead by recycling bottles, broken windshields, and any other shattered glass to make Krobo beads. In Burkina Faso, plastic prayer mats are recycled into colorful bracelets. Bronze jewelry turns green these days in Mali, where abandoned bronze radiators are pounded out and transformed into earrings

FOOD

WORLD CUISINE IS BEST EATEN FROM A STREET CART. Seek out traditional dishes, avoid the familiar arches and Java, and don't be afraid to wrap your taste buds around the absurd. In our most delicious chapter, you'll learn how to get down with crêpes in iconic France, masses of meat in Argentina, and pizza in Italy. We threw a few chicken fetuses (Vietnam), sheep's heads (Iceland), fried ants (Chiapas, Mexico), and baby mice (Korea) into the mix as a crunchy top layer of food exploration fun. Your stomach may be angry with you when all is said and eaten, but sampling authentic local food is a great way to dive into local culture, mouth-first.

Argentina

MEAT-EATER'S GUIDE TO MEAT-EATING

IN ARGENTINA, THERE ARE more cows roaming the countryside than there are people. With more than fifty million bovine grass-munchers, it's no surprise that Argentina is one of the world's biggest beef consumers, with each meat-loving citizen consuming an average of 247 pounds of cow per year. Use our guide to chow with the best of them . . . and apologize to your colon later.

Get Your Gauchos in Order

Beef is more than food in Argentina, it's a way of life—just ask any of the burly cowboys, or *gauchos*, who tend the cattle. Back in the nineteenth century, gauchos were nomadic riders who wandered the plains in search of wild cattle. Their knowledge of the land and horse-handling skills made them a hot commodity in the Argentine army. They were instant heroes, and the image of a poncho-clad, pistol-wielding, spur-wearing gaucho is the ultimate symbol of Argentine identity. In addition to pumping patriotism into the heart of every countryman, these guys have inspired an entire nation to protein-load like it's no one's business. *Asado*, the gaucho way of cooking a hand-butchered cow, is a national pastime akin to a pig roast in the American South. Today, the term gaucho has evolved to describe pretty much any dude from the Pampas with a cow.

Chew On This!

Figuring out what to order at a *parilla* (steakhouse) can be a bit tricky, especially if your Spanish is no bueno. Here are a few key phrases to get you started—let your drooling taste buds do the rest:

PICADA

A typical cheese and cold cut appetizer plate that usually comes with salami, chorizo, pâté, cured ham, green and black olives, assorted fine cheeses, and French bread. Most legit bars will serve picada, so order a plate to prep your innards for the incoming feast.

PARILLA COMPLETA

Can't make up your mind on what to order? Try a bit of everything with the *parilla completa*, a sampler mega-entrée of steak, chicken, *morcilla* (blood sausage/black pudding), *chorizo* (sausage), *mollejas* (sweetbreads—word to the wise: not bread), *riñones* (kidneys), and *chinchulines* (intestines). Bonus points if you can polish off a side order of *papas fritas* (fries).

BIFE DE LOMO

This juicy tenderloin is the most expensive cut you can get at a parilla. Fanatics, however, often complain that it doesn't taste as good as it looks due to a lack of marbling—the lines of fat within a steak that dissolve into a buttery goodness when cooked. Eat it, then judge.

ASADO DE TIRA

If you're a carnivore on a tight budget, get an order of these crispy short ribs on the cheap. You might want to invest in some floss, though—the downside is that you'll probably spend the next few hours slyly prying stray pieces from your teeth.

BIFE DE CHORIZO

A meat-lover's favorite, this cut of sirloin (New York strip) looks and tastes so good that no sauce is necessary, as your drool will be moisture enough. Better plan on wearing stretchy pants or loosening your belt one notch.

ENTRAÑA

If you're new to the meat scene, go for an *entraña*. Although this local favorite is cut pretty thin, it packs a ton of flavor. The fact that it won't clog your arteries as fast as a bife de lomo or bife de chorizo is a plus. Don't let protein-deficient American veg-heads get you down; even the meatiest of meat-lovers can find safety in Argentina. Just remember to keep a bottle of Pepto on hand to tame that meat beast once it hits your stomach.

Temperature Tip

WHEN ORDERING A STEAK, keep in mind that Argentine steakhouses will usually slightly overcook your meat. Here is the essential terminology to get your meat just the way you like it.

Vuelta y vuelta—Super rare, or "blue" in foreign meat lingo.
Jugoso—Rare (or "juicy," literally)
Medio—Medium-rare
A punto—Medium-well
Bien cocido—Well-done

Chiapas

NOT A TACO BELL IN SIGHT

WAY MORE THAN THE bastardized burritos and nachos you pick up at window #2, Mexican food is such a big deal, the cuisine was named by UNESCO as an intangible cultural heritage of mankind. Spicy, tangy, and full of rich soul, the Chiapas region is also the cheapest in all of Mexico, making all its edibles available to you at street-food prices.

Elote

In Chiapas, it all starts with corn, a sacred crop deeply embedded in Mayan culture and considered a gift from the gods. *Elote* (corn on the cob) is a major street food and is usually grilled, then super-slathered in mayo. To layer flavor on your natural stick of Mexican food history, other topping options include chili powder, butter, salt, grated cotija cheese, salsa picante, and lemon or lime juice. If picking corn out of your teeth on the streets gets grueling, check out elote's loose cousin, *esquite*, an off-the-cob version served in a bowl with a mixture of the above ingredients and eaten with a spoon.

OTP TIP: Add some corn to your corn by chugging down *pozol*, a drink made of corn dough and water (*pozol blanco*), or mixed with cacao (*pozol de cacao*), and popular during Mayan ceremonies where it was believed to help the Indígenas make long journeys through the jungle. When your corn baby fully matures, flush and don't look down.

Nucú

Why yes, those are curled up ant legs on your plate. A Chiapas specialty, Nucú (aka chicatana) are essentially oversized queen ants filled with thousands of eggs. Usually roasted and salted, served with lime juice and chile powder, and sometimes sprinkled on tacos (if you like an extra crunch). Nucú mate in swarm-orgies every June, after which all the males die, leaving bloated females to sit around until dinnertime. Best to take off their head and direct your bite straight at their fat asses.

Lengua

If your own tongue just ain't cutting it anymore, Chiapas is your mouth's chance to get real personal with beef tongue. Rubbing taste buds with a cow may sound like twisted bestiality, but the meat is chewy, with a dense, smooth texture and not half bad taste-wise. You can find a lickin' in burritos and tacos, or on its own with a sauce.

Try it with saffron sauce (*lengua en salsa de azafran*) to make you, and your new beefy friend, salivate.

Tacos

Instead of giving you our gringo taco banter, while in Chiapas, OTP was lucky enough to meet Jesús Catalán, the self-proclaimed "Taco King," and he's better equipped to give you the deep insider view of Mexico's favorite sandwich. Catalán is legit: Born in Del Valle, the taco epicenter of Mexico City, he has consumed millions of tacos around the world and, after seventeen years, still holds the record for eating the most Tacos de Canasta (sixty-three) in a single sitting.

So, what makes a good taco? Catalán says it's all about "tortillas, beans, chile, the fresh ingredients of a salsa, and the essential squeeze of lime." He's willing to get on an airplane for his Chiapan taco fix: DIY taco joints (*puestos*) at the shore of Lago Pojol in El Parque Nacional Lagunas de Montebello, " . . . there you'll find homemade fresh cheese wrapped in banana leaves, that will be grilled and topped with black beans, chorizo, and avocado slices. Ask for tortillas and make tacos, those are really authentic." Catalán swears that, "God is a taquero, life is a puesto, love is the salsa, and you are the taco." To Catalán, tacos in Chiapas are a big deal, and he's ready to wage war on anyone trying to mess with his favorite street eats. In fact, he " . . . dare[s] anyone with a passion for tacos to bring it on and try to steal [his] crown." You hear that? *Be* the taco.

Tamales

These are not your freezer section logs of awful. Chiapas' nutty version, called *tamales chiapanecos*, are a regional creation. They come wrapped in banana leaves and filled with pork, raisins, tomatoes, almonds, onions, and spicy herbs. The dough contains chipilín, an herb native to Chiapas that gives these tamales a little extra flair. Purchase yours from any guy peddling them from his bike. Super-agriculturalists since before America was "born," you best believe the people of Chiapas know their shit when it comes to food. The Taco King will tell you: "In such a diverse country as Mexico, food is perhaps the strongest element that 'glues' us all. Old and young, rich and poor, religious or not." Combine that with the "*mi casa es su casa*" mentality, and you got yourself a street feast worth a trip way south of the border.

France

CRÊPE YOUR PANTS IN FRANCE

FRENCH FOOD GIVES US A *boner appétit.* From their locally grown food, picked-fresh from their diverse landscapes, to their willingness to eat anything and everything, the French are true chefs, who make everyone else look like lowly line cooks. Even back in the Middle Ages, when royalty from neighboring countries wanted a special feast, they ordered out from France, in what was probably the slowest delivery service ever. Crêpes are the centerpiece of French cuisine and can be eaten anywhere, at any time, and on any budget.

The Skinny on Crêpes

Crêpes are pretty simple—pour a thin layer of batter on a skillet and cook until it's like a giant, ultra-thin pancake. Then throw whatever ingredients you want on top and wrap it up.

Sweet Crêpes

Super-thin, white sheets of lightly sweetened wheat flour are stuffed with fruit, jam, or any sort of sugary filling or spread. Nutella is a favorite—a hazelnut spread that, in the rest of the world, has made peanut butter its bitch. Go sweet for breakfast, dessert, or some post-toke munchies.

Savory Galettes

A "dark meat" variation, galettes are made with unsweetened, darker buckwheat batter and filled with anything from veggies and cheese to beef burgundy for a cheap lunch or dinner. Smelly French cheese melted all over earthy mushrooms are the way to go if you're looking for a galette to whet your appetite.

All Crêpe-d Out

Throw ice cream on it, and you have crêpe à la mode. Set Grand Marnier on fire, pour it on top, and you have crêpe suzette. Roll it up like a cigar, bake it, and have it with afternoon tea for crêpe dentelle. Stack a dozen crêpes on top of one another with filling in between each, and you have a mille crêpe cake. And in traditional French fashion, be sure you wash it all down with some alcoholic cider.

Creep Up on Crêpes

Crêpes are the food of choice for poor Parisians, so *crêperies* are as prevalent there as titties are on a French beach. Find them near the starving artists in Montmartre and broke college students in the Latin Quarter. The best spot to get crêpes, though, is their birthplace in Brittany, France. When those crêpe chefs traveled to Paris, they set up shop just outside the Montparnasse train station, where they still whip up the best crêpes in town.

National Crêpe Day

FEBRUARY 2 IS NATIONAL CRÊPE DAY! IT IS SAID THAT IF YOU can catch a crêpe with a frying pan after tossing it in the air with your right hand while holding a gold coin in your left, you will become rich that year. Before you start making any judgments about this tradition, remember that you spent that same day watching a rodent crawl around a pen and believe its actions could somehow have an impact on the global climate for the next six weeks. We'd rather eat crêpes.

Iceland

SURF AND TURF WITH WINGS

THE LOBSTER, STEAK, AND chicken platter in Iceland is a little different. Their "surf" is bigger, their "turf" is badder, and their "wings" are international icons. Living in a fairly remote island nation, Icelanders have historically eaten some weird-ass shit to sustain themselves. Here are three pickings to shock your palate.

Surf
Whale: The Other Red Meat

A beached whale is normally a sad scene. You think about *Free Willy* and wonder how the world can be so cruel, tossing this majestic being out of its waters to perish on the hot shore. While you play out the sob story in your head, Icelanders come a runnin' with forks and knives. The Minke whale is popular in Icelandic cuisine and, while it's usually served grilled or on a skewer, can be fancied-up and eaten sashimi-style.

Turf
Deep in Sheep

Forget your chef's knife; to prepare Svið, you'll need a saw. This traditional Icelandic dish is prepared by first singeing off all remaining fur on a sheep's head, sawing it in half through the brains and down the jaw, then tossing the sucker with some salt, and throwing it in a pot to slow simmer. All kinds of superstitions exist around eating the various parts of the head, especially the ears, and the eyeballs are said to be finger-lickin' good. Normally served with much more tame sides (like mashed potatoes), this turf fare is available at both cheap eats and high-end restaurants.

Wings
Puffins

Gracing the covers of cereal boxes everywhere, chubby, penguin-like puffins are native to Iceland. You may have crunched down on their carb-y breakfast products, but Icelanders used to eat the real deal until the lovable bird population steeply declined. You may find some off-the-books puffin dishes flapping around the outskirts of the island, but for the most part, these birds are now reserved for picture-taking and not devouring.

Fermented Booze: Brennivin

HOW COULD YOU GO WRONG WITH A DRINK KNOWN AS "BLACK Death"? Brennivín, which appropriately translates to "burning wine," is the signature drink in Iceland. This concoction of fermented potato mash with caraway seeds, cumin, and angelica tastes like rye bread soaked in gasoline. You won't find an Icelander with an income drinking it, so who does? Budd from *Kill Bill*, David Grohl in a song where he's turning to "Skin and Bones," and Icelandic bums and others with similar finances and hygiene (aka *you*).

Pagan Food Fest

ÞORRABLÓT (OR THURSEBLOT, IN CASE YOU'RE NOT ONE OF the eleven or so people who speak Icelandic) is a festival held in mid-January, when the locals get sick of being bitch-slapped by the frost. Dedicated to Thor, a Norse god associated with everything that's stormy and terrible, this food-focused celebration begs him to hammer back the winter and let the spring warm the island. The first day of Thurseblot is called *Bóndadagur*, or "Husband's Day," and traditionally, women bring the men breakfast in bed—just as the men will do on *Konudagur*, "Woman's Day" (if they know what's good for them).

Most Icelanders celebrate Thurseblot at home with friends, but you can find some restaurants serving traditional foods, as well. Far from pumpkin pies and roasted brussels sprouts, to do it up viking style, slurp some ram testicles or chow down on *lundabaggar*, a sausage made from the butcher's leftovers (like colons), which are then rolled up, boiled, pickled, and sliced. No ranch dressing for dipping either, so nut up and swallow.

Continue feasting on the go by gnawing on a chunk of dried and fermented *Hákarl* jerky—a fish that doesn't have a bladder so it pisses out of its skin. Another delicacy is selshreifar, or seal flippers, which are generally cured in lactic acid and taste like thick, chewy milk.

Italy

ITALIAN FOOD FIGHT: NORTH VS. SOUTH

WAY BEFORE HIPSTERS AND food evangelists cornered the term "locavore," Italians were munching on food picked from their yard, slaughtered in their kitchen, and caught at the bubbling streams outside their windows. The best food in the north or south is generally what grows well in the micro-climate of that region. Italians like to keep their sons (*cough*) mama's boys (*cough*) and their food close to home. Northern Italy borders Switzerland, Austria, and France, so food there has more French and German influences than in the South, which is warmer and surrounded by the sea. As such, asking a northern Italian for lasagna (a southern dish) should elicit some unpleasant hand gestures. Read up on the great food divide so you can food-slut your way around Italy without any nasty bumps.

Dirty South

If your privates get public when you think about pizza and pasta, head down to the south, where their giant, juicy tomatoes make the Catholic schoolgirls blush. If you're gonna bust buttons on one city's streets, let it be Naples. More than anywhere else in Italy, Naples will pound you proper with its sweet dough and cheese. After tearing into a pizza at a standby, like L'Antica Pizzeria da Michele, make your sweet tooth ache at the many kiosks and tiny open-storefront bakeries. Get good and creamed with *zeppoli* (deep-fried dough balls, often filled with sweetened ricotta, pastry cream, or custard) and *sfogliatelle* (crunchy, pleated shell-shaped pastries usually filled with sweet ricotta). If you end up with custardy dribbles on your chin, so be it.

Naughty North

If you dig cooler temps, cabbage and kale, and some blue-eyed blondes with your Italian food, head up north, where the government isn't fucked up, and food is less likely to put you in a carb coma. In Venice, all that creeping around on canals has given the locals a taste for funked-out fish. *Baccalà mantecato* is salted, sometimes dried, creamed cod. Venetians pile into cramped *osterie* or *bàcari* (wine bars, often with snacks), where there's just enough room for *cicchetti* (appetizers). Served on toasty crostini, *baccalà* is a no-mayo-doused tuna fish sandwich. The cream is just the fish, pulverized and whipped into salty submission.

The Florentines, on the other hand, have been straight tripping since the fifteenth century, when peasants started getting down with all four cow stomachs. You'll know you're turning Italiano when you've acquired a taste for tripe—essentially, cattle stomach lining, which tastes just as rubbery as it sounds. If cow guts aren't your thing, chow down on *ribollita*, a black cabbage, root vegetable, and white bean soup that tastes like it's been blessed by the Pope.

Peace with Cheese

No discussion on Italian food would be complete without the lowdown on cheese. Ask the locals where to find the best cheese, and they'll respond, *"che il formaggio* (which cheese)?" If you're Italian, the world would end if your mozzarella came from the same city as your *parmigiano*—the two different regions produce two seriously different *formaggio*. The best *buffala mozzarella* is from the southern Campania region, and the best parmigiano is, wait for it, in Parma (up north).

Italians get a little Godfathery if you're ignorant about the food culture, so unless you want to find yourself dragged under a gondola or buried five-feet-deep in a Sicilian graveyard, we suggest you stop yapping and start swallowing that salami.

Korea

CHEERS TO DRINKING DEAD RODENTS!

STEP UP TO THE BAR FOR A drink fit for *Fear Factor*. As if kimchi, deer antler stew, and barbecued blowfish weren't enough, the Koreans have taken it up a few gross notches. Definitely not for the faint of heart, baby mouse wine is essentially a squinty-eyed Stuart Little shoved in a bottle and corked up tight until you're ready to drink rodents.

Why, Oh Why?

The Koreans treat this dare-to-taste drink as a cure-all health tonic. Do you have a better way to cure everything from asthma to liver disease

with a quick swig? Neither do we, so put a mouse in it and drink up. The Koreans (and the Chinese) have been gagging on it for decades.

The Process: Mousification

Quite simple: take wine, add baby mice to it, and get baby mice wine. Now let's get down to the specifics. The end of the road (for those slimy

rodents) and the beginning of your experience starts with rice wine. The first thing to hit your lips better be good, 'cause the pile of mice that follows doesn't seem so pleasurable. Close to sake, but not quite, this stuff's pretty strong with nearly twice the alcohol of regular grape wines. As for the mice, these poor little rodents are just a day or two old, ripped straight from mama's teat, and shoved into the bottle to test their swimming capabilities. Sadly, none survive, and all are left to garnish the bottom of the bottle, which sits on a shelf for at least one year. This is the holy fermentation period, during which the magically miraculous health benefits of baby mice swirl around the wine and give this Korean concoction its body.

Strong Notes of Whisker

Head to a specialty drink shop and pick up a squeaky bottle. Baby mice are used because they don't have any fur, but one swig of this stuff is sure to put some hair on your chest. Your first sip is going to blow you back with raw gasoline flavor, but like any serious drink, the shots get easier as you go along. Once all the liquid is gone, tip that bottle over and chow down on some fine, fermented mouse. To ensure that nobody will approach you for miles, hit it with a side of kimchi to create an impenetrable force field of gross smells and sights.

Smells Awful, Tastes Great!

SAY KIMCHI! KOREANS DOWN SO MUCH OF THIS SWEATY-
sock-smelling dish that they swap "kimchi" for "cheese" when they smile for photos. A super-spicy and delicious condiment that dubs as a main dish, kimchi is just fermented cabbage or radish mixed with garlic, salt, vinegar, chili peppers, anchovies, and other paint-peeling spices. Wipe that disgusted look off your face, fellas. Kimchi may smell like an unkempt Korean kookah, but it's packed with vitamins and is here to stay.

Georgia

HOW TO EAT YOUR WEIGHT IN BREAD

THERE'S NOTHING GEORGIA- peachy about the street food in this former part of the Soviet Union. The Republic of Georgia has spent some seventy years cut off from the rest of the world, eating bread and cheese in every combination possible. Pick up all the delicious crumbs behind the Iron Curtain and bloat yourself into oblivion on the republic's kick-ass street cuisine.

Khachapuri

Bread and cheese: those two crazy kids go together like awesome and sauce. Georgians peddle this cheesy bread heaven—called *khachapuri*— across the country. The versions range from cheese-stuffed to cheese-topped and from flaky to über-bready. In the beach town of Batumi, things really get out of control with a boat-shaped variety filled with egg, butter, cheese, and more cheese. Forget pizza and quesadillas, Georgians are the iron chefs of artery-clogging.

Tonis Puri

Carb dieters may as well jump off one of the country's massive mountain ranges if they plan to avoid bread in the ex-commi country. Seeing locals walk the streets stuffing their faces with fresh flatbread (*tonis puri*) is about as common as hookers in Bangkok— and maybe equally as tempting. To get on the carb bandwagon, look for the typical hole-in-the-wall bakeries marked with the word "t'one." Pronounced "toe-nay," this means the bakery is equipped with an old-school clay oven that pops out hot bread all day.

Khinkali

Save up some cash and splurge on a sit-down meal to try one of the country's most famous dishes: *khinkali*. Essentially fatty dim sum, the doughy-pouched dumplings are a spiced-meat-and-oozy-juice party in your mouth. Unlike their Chinese counterpart, these more gigantic versions are served in mass quantities to satisfy even the most raging case of the munchies.

OTP TIP: To eat it like the locals, first slurp up the liquid insides by holding the *khinkali* by the top and taking a bite from the bottom.

Lobiani

Just when you thought you could totally live without refried beans, Georgia reignites your gassy passion for the cafeteria slop. The country's answer to the bean burrito—*lobiani*—comes stuffed, yet again, in more bread. All that's missing is some tequila and a side of guac.

Kada

Basically just piecrust coiled up for easy inhaling purposes, this buttery pastry is usually served at stands and bakeries. Expect it to go straight to your ass.

Cut through the Carbs with Kebab

Georgia's version of cheap street food looks like your typical lump of mystery meat but gets its local flare from a mixture of cilantro and unique spices. Down your kebab with a side of tomato sauce called *satsebeli*. With other meaty dishes, though, opt for tkemali—an herbalicious plum sauce that Georgians equate to ketchup. Eating a kebab is a great way to add a little protein to that monster loaf baking in your stomach.

Wine

If bread is the go-to grub, then wine is the go-to booze—Georgians actually claim they invented it and famously toast endlessly with the homemade, unfiltered concoction, which is a murky yellow in color. While more refined wines exist, the homebrew version is popular at most restaurants.

Fizzy Drink

No matter how nice the porcelain is, always expect a hangover after a night of drinking bathtub wine. Borjomi, Georgia's miracle mineral water, collects five miles underground as a byproduct of earth's magma, and volcanic gas bubbles it slowly upward, picking up minerals along the way and mixing it with ground water. A mile beneath the surface, the long journey ends as it feeds into Borjomi's spring wells. Borjomi is said to boost the immune system, ease digestive issues, increase metabolism, prevent cavities, replenish electrolytes, treat diabetes, and of course, cure hangovers. So, when you're suffering from the wrath of this country's unfiltered grapes, know that Mother Earth has been cooking up your cure for 1,500 years.

Stroke This! Churchkhela

SO EATING SOMETHING THAT RESEMBLES a dildo covered in anal beads won't be weird at all, right? The Georgians don't think so. This funky little joystick has been coined the "Georgian Snickers"— what with its hand-held convenience and nutty interior. Don't expect it to be all sweet and chocolaty, though. Instead, the Eurasian street-treat—often found in other countries throughout the region—tastes more like nuts covered in a fruit roll-up.

Vietnam

BAHN YOURSELF PHO REALS!

A FEW YEARS BACK, VIET- namese cuisine was something only its people and a small handful of food-savvy non-Asians knew much about. Today, it has become one of the trendiest stateside ethnic foods. While any Yelp-user can whip up a list of hipster-packed "authentic" Vietnamese restaurants in Seattle, Santa Ana, or Houston, why not one-up those PBR-guzzlers by hightailing it to the motherland instead?

Bahn

Any food item containing the word "banh" means it's flour-based, and there's no better way to kick-start the day than with a huge plate of carbs. Out of all the yeasty treats, the most popular is the *banh mi*, a crispy baguette stuffed with your choice of cold cuts, grilled or roasted pork, pâté, pickled carrots and daikon, cilantro, chili peppers, cucumbers, buttered mayo, eggs, or all of the above.

Another popular *banh* variety is the *banh xeo*, a giant savory Vietnamese crepe packed with fatty pork, shrimp, mint leaves, basil, and bean sprouts, pan-fried over a charcoal burner and topped off with *nuoc mam* (that delicious, foul-smelling fish sauce).

Available at all banh xeo-only restaurants on Tuyen Quang St. (aka Banh Xeo Street) in Phan Thiet, listen for the loudest sizzles to pick your dispensary.

noodle soup comes loaded with marinated beef, sliced cabbage, raw onions, oxtail, pork knuckles, and congealed pig's blood—if you're no Bourdain, you can ask them to hold the last two.

Pho Sho!

Forget that shitty Ramen you lived on as a starving college kid. When it comes to noodles, the Vietnamese don't mess with that cup-o-junk. Instead, warm up your spoon for some *pho* (pronounced "fuh" not "foh"), a steaming-hot bowl of vermicelli noodle soup served with beef or chicken, bean sprouts, basil, and cilantro. Spice it up with some chili peppers, a squirt of lime juice, and Sriracha.

If your broth ends up a bright red from all that Sriracha, congrats! You've graduated to *bun bo hue*, a spicier, sassier pho variety from central Vietnam. This lemongrass-laden

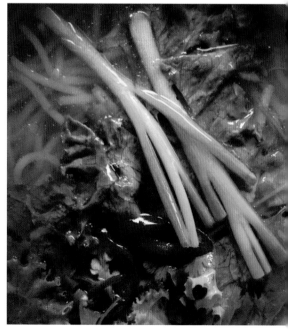

Roll Up

For a light midday snack, grab some *goi cuon*, or spring rolls. The main ingredients—pork, shrimp, lettuce, vermicelli noodles, and fresh herbs— are wrapped in delicate rice paper and served in a neat, easy-to-manhandle bundle. Dip it in some peanut hoisin sauce and avoid looking vulgar as you shove it in your mouth whole.

Test Your Gag Reflexes

EVEN ANDREW ZIMMER would have a hard time swallowing some of the outrageously gnarly shit Asians choke down. Consuming a pseudo-fetus is probably frowned upon by most Americans, but it's totally the norm in Southeast Asia. Locals eat the shit out of fertilized duck and chicken eggs, known as *trung vit lon* in Vietnam. How it's done: Take a partially incubated egg, boil it for twenty minutes, crack it open with a spoon, and enjoy the savory flavor of an aborted bird fetus. These wildly popular embryonic treats are typically sold by rowdy street vendors and are a late-night favorite among drunken revelers. Forget all the other weird stuff they hawk on the streets down there; *trun vit lon* is the ultimate food challenge and comes with foodie bragging rights (as long as you omit the part about your puking feathers all afternoon).

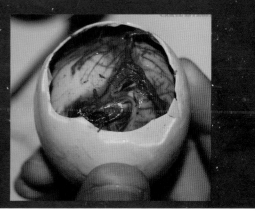

Sweets

Feed your food baby one last time with some che, a dessert beverage or pudding usually made with some variation of fruit, beans, and sticky rice. One of the most commonly consumed is *che sam bo luong*, a sweet, cold soup made with lotus seeds, sliced seaweed, red jujubes, dried longans, Job's tears, and crushed ice.

Finish Off with a Cold One

Vietnamese people aren't big drinkers in general (damn that Asian red-face-inducing, lack-of-alcohol-digestion gene!), but they still know how to enjoy a drink or two. Each region has a local draft beer named after it (Bia Saigon, Bia Can Tho, etc.), and deciding which one's best comes down to the drinker's own taste. If price outweighs taste, the cheapest beer in the land is Bia Hoi, at sixteen cents a pint.

Snake Village

FOR A SPECIAL EVENING OUT, GRAB A GLASS
of *ruou ran*, or snake wine. Take your pick of steeped
wine, where snakes are soaked in the wine for several
months before it is served, or mixed wine, in which the
snake gets sliced down the belly and its blood is drained
into a delicious shot glass of wine. Don't worry—ethanol
in the wine denatures the snake venom, so you won't
have to call a medic. Hit up one of the many slithery
snake wine bars in Le Mat (or Snake Village) outside of
Hanoi. Fang-fucking-tastic!

MUSIC

EVERY COUNTRY HAS DISTINCT MUSICAL ROOTS, AND GLOB-alization has remixed the world's music scene into some interesting sounds. From regional musical superstars, globally intertwined genres, live festivals, and the busking culture, the music of the world is best experienced live. Pick up a fiddle and jam in Belfast with the drunkest musicians on the planet, or shed a tear to the sad Fado tunes in Portugal. While we can tell you everything we know about the origins of dubstep in London, it's up to you to get out there and actually feel the bass thumping, yourself.

Belfast

SINGING WITH THE IRISH: WHEN BOOZE AND TUNES COLLIDE

MANY OF BELFAST'S PUBS have been hosting the drunk and rowdy since the seventeenth century. In these historic pubs, you can warm up and listen to traditional Irish music for free, until you're ready to join in and lend your vocal chords to a little Irish bending. You will emerge feeling like the winner of *American Idol* and smelling like an alleyway on St. Patrick's Day.

Looking for Treble Trouble

You can find Irish music almost any night of the week. Some sessions begin with a few musicians, and as the night (and the pints) go on, others will often join in. These are called "traditional sessions," and as you may expect, most musicians take a long Guinness break between every song. Occasionally, you might see a fight or a jig break out; in either case you can join in or sit back and watch.

Irish Instruments

Your Jameson-flooded eyes aren't playing tricks on you; the Irish are known to have some funky music makers. Uilleann pipes are kind of like bagpipes except the air is pumped

with the elbow instead of the mouth—sure, it looks goofy, but the Irish bust out some quality jams on these things. You also might see a pear-shaped, guitar-like instrument known as a bouzouki. This thing came to Ireland in the mid-'60s from Greece and is now a staple in Irish jigs. To round out the band, flutes, fiddles, harps, and accordions will all chime in.

Jigga Where?

Madden's has the best Guinness, features sessions almost every night, and brings in a mostly local crowd. You have to buzz the door for entry, a relic of the days when the Protestant/Unionists would attack Catholic/Nationalist pubs and vice versa. Around the corner is seedier Kelly's pub, where you won't have trouble finding a fight to go with your pint. Aside from being the oldest building in the city of Belfast, McHugh's is one of the big daddies in food and music, and has an early-bird session on Saturday afternoons. The Garrick is aces for pub grub and for catching a few football (soccer) matches before the music begins.

Drunken Irishmen and musical instruments are the hallmark of any successful trip to the Emerald Isle. If you haven't hugged a few leprechaun-lovers, sung yourself into hoarse oblivion, and drunk enough Guinness to turn your stomach into an Easy-Bake Oven by the end of your trip, stock up on lucky charms and try again.

DUBSTEP OR DIE

DUBSTEP IS DIFFICULT TO

describe, but its intention is clear—to remind you of your mortality. When your heart begins grinding to the rhythm of reverberating bass, you'll know that you're stepping right up to the dub. It's not techno; it's not grime; it's not dnb—it crosses all of those. Some call it noise, while others swear it's a life-altering musical experience. Our philosophy is simple: If it moves you, then fuck it, just move.

DubStart

Dubstep was born in London circa 2002 from the fusion of the various glimmers of electronica available at the time, paired with deep basslines drawn from Jamaican reggae styles. Early dub had no room for vocals or melodies. Instead, artists focused on building up existing genres like jungle, techno, and house with spine-rattling

drum and bass, looping already looped and sampled recordings and working everything into a head-boppin', epilepsy-inducing, musical mega scene. Dubstep became a movement of bass fiends that crowded London's dance clubs enough for the mainstream to do a double take. Then Skrillex and his "My Little Gothic Pony" hair came prancing along and spread his version of the genre to the American audience, much to the angry dismay of many U.K. dub-lovers.

DubStep's Finest

Forget Skrillex; let's talk about the U.K. greats. Sending the sales of subwoofers through the roofers, Skream and Benga are the highly respected PlayStation pioneers of the genre and are often credited with bringing dubstep to the public ear. Caspa, from West London, is well known for fusing some pop to the step by setting Top-40 tracks to dubstep beats. Flux Pavilion, a one-dude operation, hopped on the scene in 2008 and has since made a booming thump, with Jay-Z and Kanye taking notice (and borrowing beat samples) in 2011. But it's not just about lone dub do-gooders. Many producers and artists collaborated to transform their individual styles and come up with collective new beats to bring to the table.

Let the Beat Drop

Finding a London dubstep club that will rock you till your teeth chatter isn't difficult. Plastic People is one of the best places to step on the toes of other bass whores. It's small, dark, sweaty, and you'll feel your cellulite jiggling to the rhythm. Tucked under the arches of the London Bridge, the club Cable evokes feelings of being bent over and reamed with bass continually until you tap out. It's intense, and the party goes well into the morning—it continues until 1 p.m. on Sunday. One of London's best-known venues, Fabric, is big, grimy, and mostly a sausage party (great for the ladies!). Fabric is an institution for Friday night dubstep raves with live acts, but you should know that the floor is rigged to vibrate with the music, so stabilize your ankles and let the bass possess you.

Our technological era has made it so that just about anyone can be a dubstep artist. But as the saying goes, just because you *can*, doesn't mean you *should*. Let the professionals in London dub your ass to death instead.

The World's Most Poppin' Music Venues

NO NEED TO HOLD YOUR IPOD EARBUDS DEEP INTO YOUR EARS
any longer. Pack a lighter and hop on the OTP tour bus; these venues will crank up the volume to a level you've never heard before.

SLANE CASTLE, IRELAND—Situated along the River Boyne, this castle's grounds sport enough room for 80,000 loyal tune junkies to get their high-quality fix.

SYDNEY OPERA HOUSE, AUSTRALIA—Like the Eiffel Tower is to France, this award-winning arts building has become the face of Australia. Don't let the name fool you; there's plenty of awesome music to munch on other than opera.

RED ROCKS AMPHITHEATER, COLORADO—Sandwiched between two 300-foot sandstone rocks, Red Rocks' stage was built by Mother Nature and approved by countless music-loving humans.

02 ARENA, LONDON—The unofficial king of music venues, 02 constantly competes for the reigns with Madison Square Garden of New York City. This gold-standard stadium is situated on the grounds that hosted London's Olympic games in 2012.

DALHALLA, SWEDEN—A rockin' venue made entirely of rocks, Dalhalla soundtracks summertime in Sweden. The thin moat that separates the stage from the crowd means you better bring a board if you intend to crowd surf.

Portugal

WHAT THE F*CK IS FADO?

FADO, LITERALLY TRANS- lated, means prophecy, fate, or destiny. Culturally, it is known as the "soul of Portugal." A heart-wrenching form of musical poetry, Fado is a style of song that came out of tiny Portugal's big-shot days, when explorers set off to sea to discover new lands while the women they left behind longingly wailed across the water, awaiting their return. If you're ever feeling homesick abroad, stop being a pussy and find some solidarity with Fado.

Sounds Like . . .

Influenced by former Portuguese colonies—as well as North African jams—and blended with Portuguese poetry and urban folk tradition, the music is haunting and evocative (something like a blend of mellow Hawaiian tunes and Flamenco), and embraces the concept of *saudade*, roughly interpreted as "melancholy." The vocals are traditionally backed by a twelve-string Portuguese guitar that looks like a knocked-up banjo.

Hey, Who Fado-ed?

Portugal wasn't always so embracing of Fado—at one point it was predominantly sung by prostitutes in brothels and considered evil. While these days you might chance on the odd sex-trade worker with a great voice and repertoire of Fado to accompany your ten-minute squeezer, you'll find legit *fadistas* singing in the Moorish Alfalma district in Lisbon. Fado performances are generally held in dimly lit taverns known as *Casas de Fado*, which are bare bones in terms of acoustics. It's considered impolite and distracting to the fadista to eat while she or he is singing, and the food at these joints tends to be on the crappy side anyway.

Poke Around Portugal

Take a road trip down to the University town of Coimbra, where the Fado has a different flavor. Coimbra Fado is more likely to be sung by a man or men (vs. women in Lisbon), and because the town is all about university smarts, the musical style is more affiliated with the intellectual class than its blue-collar counterpart in the capital. Check out the *Fado ao Centro* (Fado Center) for an inexpensive and enlightening performance. Round out your folk-music vacation in Oporto, where you can sip some thick and sweet fortified port wine. Let out the last of your sobs at *Casa da Mariquinhas*, the oldest and best-known Fado house in Oporto.

Know Your Fado

If you get into a Fado name-dropping predicament, Amália Rodrigues, who sang in the Lisbon style, is an important one to know. Early in Rodrigues' career, she began renovating Fado's melodies, modernizing them, and setting some to sixteenth-century poems by Luís de Camões. While this finagaling with the classics was criticized by many Fado traditionalists, most came to love her, and she is now considered the "Queen of Fado," as well as a national icon.

Ukraine

REPUBLIC OF KAZANTIP

JUST THE TIP WON'T DO
here. Jam it in raw in the Republic of
KaZantip—a month long state of rave
and orgy-by-the-seashore in Ukraine.
KaZantip is not a festival, like Burning
Man or those found in Ibiza. It's a
hedonistic rave-country where you
get a viZa to become a citiZen of the
craZiest nation in Eastern Europe.

HistorZ of KaZantip

Started in 1992, the Republic of
KaZantip sprung from the imagina-
tion of one man, Nikita Marshunok,
known throughout rave-nation as
"the PreZident." The largest party in
Eastern Europe started as a kitesurf-
ing competition with about eighty
competing surfers and 600 spectators. As the story goes, the preZident
set up speakers and piped in some
jams to set the groove mood for the
competition. The next year, real DJs
showed up with their own electronic
and vinyl magic, and a tradition was
born—growing in size and reputation
each year. In 1997, the PreZident
threw the annual event in KaZantip—
the site of an unused nuclear power
station—and a reactive republic of
music, sex, and hotness was born.

To Z or Not to Z?

Although not recognized as an official
nation, KaZantip has its own government, constitution, laws, and religion.
Before purchasing a viZa to become a
citiZen, all ravers are required to read
the constitution and agree to conditions like "be the one you want to be"
and "live life with no pants."

What to Expect from Z Party

KaZantip is not a sissy weekend ben-
der, but an all-out, twenty-four-hour,
month long rager hosting over 300
top DJs from around the globe.
Expect to see some of the hottest
Ukrainian girls wearing next to nothing (or nothing—clothing is optional).
Sexual harassment is a KaZantip
crime, but free, consensual lovin' is
highly encouraged.

The Biggest, Loudest, and Wildest Music Festivals Around the World

SUMMER MONTHS SET THE MOOD FOR AMPED-UP, OUTDOOR music festivals. Peep some of these world-class events and party like a rock star.

ROSKILDE: DENMARK—Over 100,000 heads rock to big-name punk, rock, and metal bands from Scandinavia and beyond in this four-day event in Denmark. ▶

ALL TOMORROW'S PARTIES: ENGLAND—No corporate sponsors? No problem. This British alternative to the almighty Glastonbury Festival doesn't draw as big of a crowd, but we like the friendly vibes that arise from performers and fans partying together.

EXIT: SERBIA—Southeast Europe's largest cultural crowd gathers in Novi Sad (Serbia's second largest city), flooding its seventeenth-century Petrovaradin fortress with over 250,000 festival-goers annually. ◀

COACHELLA: U.S.A.—Jam packed into a three-day shitshow, California's Coachella showcases everything from mainstream hip-hop to alternative and grunge.

ESSAOUIRA GNAOUA FESTIVAL: MOROCCO—This is a freebie festival where you get tons more than you pay for. The beats that flow through the sea of sound are called "Gnawa" and put the half-million-strong crowd into a happy, ready-to-dance trance.

SEX *and* PARTYING

ALL DIFFERENCES ASIDE, EVERYONE IN THE WORLD LIKES a good party (and good sex). Party under the glow of the full moon in Thailand, thumb through a huge collection of sex toys in Paris' Pigalle, and rage on to Carnaval in Brazil, the big, feathery granddaddy of street parties. Often, you don't even have to leave your hostel to party, as many places cater to the backpacker party beast that gets unleashed the minute you step on foreign territory. With so many party possibilities, the world's party scene will make stateside weekend ragers feel like weak sauce. International hookups are bound to happen, and global great times are guaranteed.

AMSTERDAM'S TOP THREE CAFÉS

YOU'RE NOT FOOLING ANY-one—even if you claim to be visiting Amsterdam for the history, or art—everyone knows you're going to stroll through the red-light district and indulge in the city's famous "coffee shops." We're all about going to the Van Gogh Museum or checking out the Anne Frank House (sobriety recommended), but hitting up a café or two is equally essential. Whether you're already a ganja fan or a green-eyed virgin, here are three cafés you need to hit hard.

Grey Area

Originally opened by a couple of American burnouts, this joint full o' joints has been going strong for more than a decade. A "mecca for American tourists," Grey Area serves up a unique vibe alongside its tasty weed. A stoner punk's dream, this café is covered with stickers of obsolete punk bands, and you can bet on hearing a lot of The Clash. The place has won twenty-one awards for its reefer over the years and remains a celebrity favorite. Willie Nelson personally recommends Grey Area for the best shit in town, and he's joined by the good stoner company of Phish, Dave Attell, and the boys of Bush. Even Flava Flav gets his weed there, and we'd all like to try whatever crazy shit he's on.

Bluebird

Bluebird is paradise for smokers and the straight-laced alike. While the place offers some phenomenal weed, there are tree-free perks as well. On the ground floor, you'll find a knowledgeable staff to give less experienced smokers a little guidance, and some delicious hash bonbons. The upstairs is equipped with comfy couches to enjoy your purchase, and there's a non-smoking section serving up weed-free food and nonalcoholic drinks. They even have sushi night on Saturdays.

De Dampkring

A congregation den for cannabis connoisseurs, *De Dampkring* is notorious for its "Orange Bud." In 1998, the stuff won four out of six Cannabis Cup finals. In addition, the decor is dramatic and trippy, with dark mahogany wood carvings, Indian statues, gold trim, mellow music— even a color-changing mushroom lamp in the center room. The shooting location for *Ocean's Twelve*, this place wins for best vibes, hands down.

OTP Bonus: Smart Shop— Conscious Dreams

Want to take it to the next level? Check out a "smart shop," where you will find pretty much every legal psychedelic you can dream of. While the country did ban 'shrooms a few years back, they didn't ban other psychedelics containing the exact same chemical that causes the hallucinogenic experience. Conscious Dreams sells herbal supplements that result in euphoric experiences similar to Ecstasy, but that are perfectly legal and more on the natural side. Unlike a lot of smart shops, Conscious Dreams has a lounge area to take your purchases for a test drive.

Super Munchies

THE LOCALS HERE HAVE CRAFTED THE MOST SATISFYING munchies cure of all. We give you The Stoner Dog. Thanks to Amsterdam, you no longer have to aimlessly wander between pizza shop and hot dog stand, deciding which one would hit the spot. The Stoner Dog is basically a pizza on top of a hot dog. Now if they sprinkled some M&Ms and a handful of Doritos on top, the world would be at peace.

Berlin

BERLIN'S BEER CULTURE: COMMUNAL DRUNKFESTS

LIKE TWINS CONJOINED AT the skull, separating Germany and beer would result in a bloody mess. Not ones to fuck around when it comes to brew, Berlin is a history-soaked place in northern Germany where beer drinking is also a varsity sport and biergartens, beer bars, and festivals provide countless options for saturation.

Frothy Culture

While the famous blond lagers have only been around for 150 years, Germans have been brewing beer for at least 3,000 years. They're so psychotic about their beer that special laws were created surrounding its production. The Reinheitsgebot, or the German Beer Purity Law, states that beer only equals water, barley, and hops. This ensures that every brewer gets a level playing field and eliminates the possibility of drinking a six-pack of elephant piss (we're looking at you, Bud Light). Despite the rigidity of what goes into their beer, the consumption laws are surprisingly lax. In Berlin, there are no open-container laws, so the U-Bahn, S-Bahn, streets, squares, parks, and everywhere in between become a virtual beer garden. That's great news for cheap travelers who want to bum it with a tallboy and skip the bars altogether.

Beer the Berlin Way

Take the class up just a half notch to fully marinade in Berlin's beer culture. Strict beerophiles go to Berlin in August. Like Oktoberfest, the Internationale Berliner Bierfestival brings together drunks from all over the world annually. It also butts-up to the Munich event, so the opportunity to get shitfaced for an entire month and annoy a large portion of the German population is alive and well. Beer chugging is basically a national sport, and putting on your beer goggles first thing in the morning is perfectly acceptable.

For the slightly more ambitious, try the Fat Tire Bike Tour, a great way to burn beer calories while pedaling your way toward more beer. You'll get to stop at a biergarten for lunch, and if you're in no mood for *spaetzle* or *weisswursts* solids, you're totally allowed to maintain a liquid diet. Loretta's Biergarten and Café am Neuen See in the Tiergarten have large trees and tons of tables with intermixed beer and food stalls, and are perfect for outdoor re-dehydration. Here, you can get nice and hammered, then rent a rowboat on the adjacent lake.

Kjost: A Cool Spot for Brews

In Kreuzberg on Oranienstrasse street, Kjost is an old bus sitting in a lot that was once a landfill and has now been converted to a delightful bar. With a random assortment of outdoor seating, including couches and tree stumps, and a Super Nintendo on the second floor of the bus (if you sit inside), you'll be hard-up to find a place that's more unique. Plus, the beer is cheaper than in most bars, so it's a win-win. There's no scarcity of beer-infused shenanigans in Berlin. So go on—make the Spree River appear a pale shade of gold, and rock out with your stein out.

When All You Want to Do Is Dance!

BERLIN IS KNOWN FOR ITS massive club scene. The more popular places (like Tresor and Berghain) are usually expensive and picky about whom they let past the door. Make the yeast in your stomach dance till the sun rises at OTP's backpacker club picks:

WHITE TRASH

The typical posh club's grimy cousin, this place has decent burgers, a club on-site, and usually, live music in the bar area. Their beer is cheap, and it's right in the middle of the city.

CASSIOPEIA

Named after a constellation, Cassiopeia has an outside garden, and the music is normally electronica or drum/bass. This place also packs a rock-climbing wall for when you decide to let drunken Indiana Jones take the reigns.

CLUB DER VISIONÄRE

Rumored to have some of the best pizza in Berlin, this Kreuzberg club is on a river barge with a mild identity crisis. Sort of a fancy club with a tinge of grungy riverside bar/restaurant, this place is perfect for grabbing a slice and swaying side to side until the drowsies set in.

Brazil

EVERYTHING YOU NEED TO KNOW ABOUT CARNAVAL

ARGUABLY THE GREATEST party on the planet, Rio's Carnaval falls right at the top of every partier's puke-bucket list. Every February or March, from the Friday until the Tuesday before Lent, thousands of bodies flock to join Rio locals (called *cariocas*) for this five-day exhibition of excess. It's easy to get lost in the chaos of colors, parades, and street parties. Let's sift through this blur of samba, skin, insomnia, and sex.

Prepare

Coming from the United States, you'll dish out at least a grand for your high-season flight down to the "Marvelous City." Hotels and hostels in Copacabana and Ipanema shake you down for at least quadruple their normal rates and often demand full-week stays. You might do better on apartment-rental sites like Airbnb.com, but unless you're lucky enough to score a couch to surf, expect to pay a pretty penny for the very little sleep you'll get. To avoid sleeping alongside the bums on N.S. Copacabana Avenue, booking early is mandatory. You'll even notice the restaurant prices are all written in chalk so owners can jack them up during the festival. There's no way around it—Carnaval is expensive. You may have to finally take a hammer to your piggy bank, but trust us, it's worth every one of those pennies. Now let's get you a party plan.

Samba Parades

Massive, mind-boggling floats, "who the fuck comes up with this shit?" costumes, gyrating g-strings, and all the samba music your eardrums can handle await you in the Sambadrome—the half-mile-long permanent parade grounds. If you've seen pictures of Carnaval, chances are they were taken in one of the neighborhood camps known as "samba schools," where cariocas somehow manage to stay relatively naked while wearing extravagant costumes. From Saturday to Tuesday, a year of preparation culminates in a ninety-minute march, during which samba schools fiercely compete for the awe of fans and the votes of judges.

Street Parties

Skip the pricey, Viagra-popper-infested black tie balls; the street parties are way more your style. In the center of these bandas and blocos, a percussion circle pumps out nonstop samba music. Brazilians shuffle their feet and shake their asses as vendors wheel around rickety coolers of cheap beer and caipirinhas. There is no dress code, so dress up, dress down, or barely dress at all. Pick up a few samba steps and join the masses (but watch your wallets!). Check out Simpatia é Quase Amor, a street festival in Ipanema, and then head out to the Lapa neighborhood for a massive street party.

Hook Up!

Start your tongue aerobics now, because these street parties are a saliva Swap-O-Rama. Young cariocas routinely make out with dozens of drooling hopefuls in a single night. All it takes is eye contact, an approach, and a few words before you are familiarizing yourself with some hot Brazilian's taste buds.

Just Can't Swing It?

If Rio's Carnaval just isn't in the budget, fret not. Carnaval is not just a Rio holiday; it's a national holiday, celebrated throughout Brazil. Street parties pop up in towns across the country with less tourism (which means lowered costs).

If timing is the issue, you can still get a Carnaval cock tease at a samba school rehearsal. Starting in August, the schools rehearse on weekend nights, with the band practicing its samba beats and the crowds warming up their shuffling feet. The entrance and drinks are cheap, and the cariocas are all too willing to welcome their new gringo friends with *beijos*.

Brazilians Have Butts in the Bag

WHILE THERE IS A LOT OF NICE ASS OUT IN THE WORLD, Brazilians always get the Booty Olympic Gold. Whether it's all that late-night samba, or just raw natural talent, these butts wipe out the competition.

Greece

OTP'S THREE FAVORITE TITTY BEACHES IN GREECE

WITH ALL OF GREECE'S beauty, lack of inhibition, and cultural love of food, it's no wonder that the country is one of the horniest in the world. Best observed topless and beachside, Greeks are a unique, fun-loving bunch. Sneak a peek at OTP's favorite Greek titty beaches.

Red Beach, Crete

Crete's best beach requires a bit of a hike to access (there's lots of nudity, so suck it up and trek on). Signs will point you toward the beach from anywhere in Matala, eventually leading you to a goat's path that you'll hike downhill for a solid fifteen minutes. Once you've made it to the beach, leave your clothes and inhibitions behind, and embrace one of Greece's greatest titty (and then some) beaches. Awesomely convenient caves that were called home by hippies in the '70s line the ocean and provide perfect seclusion for your own body-inspection station.

Paradise Beach, Mykonos

Join the masses from all over the world as they unite to celebrate life. You've heard of "letting loose"? A trip to Paradise Beach, and you might turn to liquid. The wonderful result of combining Greece's natural beauty with nonstop partying. Forget about partying like a rock star—come here to rage like a boulder supernova.

Myrtos Beach, Kefalonia

In the northwest corner of Kefalonia lies Myrtos Beach, often regarded as the best beach in Greece. At first glance, it may seem like nothing special, but its sea of shimmery water surrounded by green mountains and swallowed by a beating sun are the winning ingredients for the perfect beach. Feel free to even out your tan lines and let your eyes wander.

IN CASE YOU WERE WONDERING

GREECE HAS LEGALIZED

prostitution. If it gets to that point, you can have all your desires fulfilled for about sixty euros. Head to the hotels and bars around Omonia Square in downtown Athens. Strip clubs are also hooker hot spots, but try to avoid going in because many are clip joints. Ladies, we're almost sorry to say that male prostitution is illegal, but why buy the distillery when you can get the Ouzo for free?

Hook-Up Spots

FANCY HOTEL BARS DOMINATE

the nightlife scene in Greece. Even if you're not a boner-fied guest, your new prospect could be the key into suite 69 if you play your cards right at the swank bar. In Athens, check out Galaxy at the Hilton, where the sunset view is arguably all the sex you'll need; the backpacker-macker hot spot Hoxton, where you can hook up with your own backpacker breed; or Mike's, if karaoke is your idea of foreplay. If you absolutely must get laid but are seriously striking out, give your dominant hand a break and head to Paradise Beach on Mykonos Island. Even Jabba the Hutt manages to score there.

Laos

FLOAT ON

THE RIVER TOWN OF VANG

Vieng initially hits you with insane scenery, then gives you an inner tube, puts a beer in your hand, and pushes you down the river for two to three hours. Along the river, there are "designated stops" or, more accurately, shitty bars to refuel your buzz.

The Shitty Bar Scene

The bar scene along the river route basically consists of a wooden platform. On it is a small bar area tended to by either a little bent-over Laotian lady and/or an extremely skinny (and most definitely cracked-out) young Laotian man. They will eagerly call out "SAIBADY!" in your direction and swing a plastic soda bottle connected to a rope over their heads and out into the water for you to catch so they can "reel" you in. House music, 50-Cent, or Lady Gaga will be blasting, and handwritten signs will display the individual bar's offerings. These will usually include "whiskey and coke buckets," beer Laos (often with a complementary shot of *lao-lao*—rice wine), weed, bucket of "mushrooms," and opium. Bags of potato chips and cigarettes are also sold. Some bars have free body paint, and people get colorful or get the flag from their home country painted on them. Dance parties go down at every stop. Rope swings and high jumps into the water are also options, if the water is deep enough.

OTP TIP: A scam that involves selling tubers opium and then alerting the Laotian authorities down the river, who then demand a "bribe" to get you out of trouble, is rumored to exist.

Rinse and Repeat Properly

Before continuing the party at night, people usually "refuel" at one of the forty restaurants serving Western or Asian food while watching *Friends* or *Family Guy* continuously looped on TV.

Tube Rats

There are definitely people who hole up in this town for a week and tube every day. Usually identified by their lingering layers of body paint, bruised shins, and lacerations on exposed areas, they travel in small packs and have probably been too fucked up to figure out a proper shower.

Tubing is a great way to meet other travelers. As the trip down the river continues, everyone gets increasingly more fucked up and starts lingering longer and longer at each stop. These might be friends for life or just other party animals testing how long and loud they can howl. Do it once, maybe twice. If you linger longer, we'll be forced to call pest patrol.

Paris

CHEAP DILDOS: PARIS' FINEST SEX SHOPS

PARIS IS A CITY WHERE baguettes aren't the only phallic objects you'll find. Don't let a TSA confiscation ruin your good times. Let OTP guide you to the finest sex shops in Paris to restock your toys and trinkets so you can leave squealing "oui, oui" all the way home.

Dark Alleys

If Ron Jeremy and Jenna Jameson were to marry, their reception would look like Pigalle Place. During World War II, soldiers nicknamed the red light district "Pig Alley," as many would rabidly visit for a taste of the good stuff after months of celibacy at the barracks. Today, the area is still a sty—where people flock like pigs to shit for the purpose of buying sex toys. Pick your pleasure with an assortment of toys, peep shows, strip clubs, and other X-rated attractions.

That's the Spot

As you walk up the stairs in the middle of the Boulevard de Clichy, you'll know you hit the right spot when it starts to smell like the Playboy mansion grotto after an all-night pool party. This den of sex is located directly below the Sacré Coeur Catholic church, perfect for cleansing your Catholic guilt or, more importantly, since Sacré Coeur sits at the highest point in Paris, checking out the amazing views while testing out your recent purchases.

Tour de France

Start your sexploits by visiting the Musée de l'érotisme (Museum of Eroticism) at 72 Boulevard de Clichy. Floors one and two are penis paradise. Here, you can also find various figurines engaging in figurine sex, including tiny depictions of priests and nuns doing the nasty. The remaining floors house temporary exhibitions. After soaking up the museum culture, head to Rebecca Rils just down the street at 76–78. This supermarché érotique is a mainstream sex supermarket and attracts tourists (like your parents, which would be really awkward). The massive store is divided into four sections: DVDs, lingerie, gadgets, and shoes. The supermarché is great for basics like colorful furry handcuffs, masks, whips, nipple clamps, and chocolate sauce. For raunchier merchandise, visit Sexodrome at 23 Boulevard de Clichy. The 'drome is an adults-only Toys "R" Us, with more than 2,500 square meters of sex toys and apparatuses, freak-nasty reading material, and general filth.

Paris may be known as the city of love, but it's got more than a few kinks down at the core. Let go of the sophistication front for a bit and let Pigalle stroke your libido in every which way.

Get in on the PDA

PARIS IS PACKED WITH enough sightseeing to *le puke*, and the Seine River is notorious for being Paris' most make-out-worthy attraction. Littered with beautiful bridges that offer unmatchable, multiperspective views of the city, this river comes with a live, busker-generated sound-track to accompany your shameless groping. Hang out on the Pont Neuf and pack a picnic afterward for the Square du Vert-Galant. Then, park your lazy ass on one of the benches on the Pont des Arts; treat your eyes to the surrounding sights of the Eiffel Tower, the Louvre, and Notre Dame Cathedral; and start doing some slimy tongue push-ups.

Spain

WHAT THE F*CK IS A BOTELLÓN?

BAR IN THE CAR, BYOB, OR A hidden flask full of the strong sauce—we've all got our own budget boozing tactics. But throw in a little good weather, some strapped-for-cash youth, and a culture that likes to knock 'em back, and you've got yourself the ultimate outdoor benderfest: botellón. Where do you sign up?

The Origin

The south of Spain might be known for those stupidly hot flamenco dancers, but one of the best things to come out of the region is botellón. Literally translated as "big bottle," botellón and all its trashy glory came to life in the '80s, when small groups of working-class locals would gather in plazas to get tipsy for cheap. Given Spain's love affair with the fiesta, it's no surprise that the tradition spread through the country like herpes during freshman year. Now, younger Spaniards toast (over and over again) to drinking and socializing without breaking the bank. We agree—it's the levelheaded thing to do.

Binging Logistics

Come weekend time, from 11 p.m. to as late as 3:30 a.m., Spanish plazas, parks, and alleys fill with fourteen- to almost-thirty-year-olds looking to binge on a budget before heading to more expensive bars and clubs. Say what? Yeah, in the land of the eighteen-year-old drinking age and living in casa till you tie the knot, parents just don't keep tabs on their teens like they do back home. And rather than drinking until their feet are numb, the Latins traditionally tend to keep their shit a tad more under control.

Bring It

The bottled beverages at botellón vary, but like many important things in life, size matters. Often called *ir de litros*, or "going out for liters," large quantities are the name of the game—from beer to juice mixtures and every other absurd fusion under the scorching Spanish sun. Most famous are the *kalimotxos*—a Basque beverage of mixology genius, which combines coke and dirt-cheap red wine. The gnarly blend might not sound like a match made in heaven, but it handily shortens the distance between sober and drunk without going bankrupt.

OTP TIP: Should you run out of drinks past purchase hours, keep an eye out for the lingering foreign street vendors hawking emergency *cervezas*.

Botellón Hotspots

If you put a tracking device on any shitty bottle (or box) of Spanish alcohol, it would lead you to impromptu booze sessions taking place on university campuses across the country.

Other hotspots include the Plaza del Carmen in Barcelona and plazas throughout the La Latina, Chueca, and Malasaña neighborhoods of Madrid. But really, come Thursday night, all squares, beaches, and parks are fair game.

OTP TIP: Macro-botellón is when people text and e-mail groups across the country to meet. This turns into a swarm of drinking and saliva-exchanging. When getting smashed at bars and *discotecas* starts to lose its luster—or when the money well runs dry—hit the streets with the Spanish teens. Bring your big bottle and make yourself at home—things are gonna get *muy* sloppy.

Naked Crazy Guy

BARCELONA, SPAIN

IF YOU HAPPEN TO BE TROLLING

Barcelona for some booty, keep an eye out for this guy. Nobody knows his name, origin, or intentions, but anyone who's taken a trip to Barcelona has probably witnessed this old guy and his foot-long flaccid cockzilla freely flapping around town. He's permanently "dressed" with an underwear tattoo—a not-so-subtle "fuck you" to public nudity laws. Catch him chatting with cops, sippin' brews, posing for pictures, ramblin' down Las Ramblas, and simply hanging out.

Thailand

THE OG FULL MOON PARTY

WELCOME TO THE BIGGEST,

baddest beach party in the world. You've never had a better excuse to bust out the glow sticks and drink out of a bucket than during a full moon in Koh Phangan, Thailand. The monthly Full Moon Party is the OG beach rave—setting the standard for letting loose seaside. With up to 30,000 attendees, Haad Rin Beach continues to lure travelers who are ready and willing to shut the small Thai island down with their crazy party ways.

Gettin' the Party Started

Some say that the party started in a wooden disco by the beach. Others claim it began with a group of local fisherman celebrating a big catch and some guy's birthday. And then there's the theory that a few foreigners are responsible for the practice of dancing under the pale moonlight after taking a bunch of drugs and determining Koh Phangan was the best place in the world to throw a party on the beach (we're not arguing).

Frisky with Thai Whiskey

Sometimes a plastic cup just doesn't cut it. Instead, full-mooners opt for the multifunctional Thai bucket—essentially your own personal sand pail of blackout-inducing jungle juice. The magic mixture varies, but typically contains Sang Som rum (known as Thai whiskey), Coca-Cola, and some Thai Red Bull to keep you strong-like-bull all night long. Bucket-binge wisely, because Thai Red Bull packs significantly more punch than the American version. Pick your poison among the never-ending line of shouting vendors and incoherently worded signs. Purchasing the bucket spares you travel time to the bar; no interruptions means more ass shaking.

Rock Hard

RUB EITHER OF THESE (OR BOTH) FOR GOOD FUCK-LUCK

or consult them if times get flaccid.

GRANDFATHER ROCK

GRANDMOTHER ROCK

Never Enough Neon

No good rave is complete without neon glow sticks. And maybe the only thing better than waving neon glow sticks is dousing oneself in neon paint—which makes it easier to see and be seen at night on the beach. Partygoers prep by covering themselves in more bright colors than an '80s prom.

OTP TIP: Buy glow paint early—that shit runs out like water at Burning Man. Also, to minimize the beer gut, apply paint to areas less prone to jiggle.

The Deets on Drugs

There's a reason that neon paint is so popular—most partygoers are trippin' balls. Between the weed-hawking reggae bars and the famous mushroom-shake-maker, Mellow Mountain, there's definitely enough of the fun stuff to go around. But beware: Word on the beach is that undercover cops keep tabs on the rowdy crowd and will arrest offenders at the drop of a Thai-bucket straw. Play it safe-ish.

OTP TIP: Can't plan your itinerary around astronomy? Hit up the Half Moon Party, or even the Black Moon Party, which take place (surprise!) during the half moon and new moon of each month.

The Treehouse

WITH ITS HIPPY VIBE AND STRAW BEACH HUTS, THE TREE-house in Kochang feels more like a co-op straight out of *The Beach* than a hostel. But guests don't come to The Treehouse for R&R; they come for the nightly dance parties and buckets of alkie. These parties are for guests, suckers staying somewhere else, *and* locals.

Part Two

GET YOUR SHIT TOGETHER

SPONTANEITY IS THE BEAUTY OF BACKPACKING, but to maximize your time, money, and experience abroad, you must first put in a little planning legwork. This section sorts out everything you need to know about getting your shit together to make the most out of your trip. You'll need to figure out where you're going and for how long; construct a budget (and loosely stick to it); book the flight out; and pin down some initial sleeping arrangements. From there, you'll get your backpack, necessary docs, and vaccines. To make this process easier, we've laid out the practical essentials and added some useful tips to get you the fuck out of here as fast as possible.

PLANNING *and* RESEARCH

IF YOU'VE NEVER TRAVELED INDEPENDENTLY BEFORE, YOUR primary concern may be cost related—around $1,000 per month is a fair medium estimate for a backpacker's monthly budget. This estimate should keep you fed, clothed, and with a roof over your head in any country around the world. (As some places are cheaper than others, you will be surprised at how much you can do on this small budget.) There are, of course, many other variables to consider, including pre-trip expenses. If money is still your main concern, head over to Money and Budgeting (page 135) to start building your budget. Just remember the old rule: Take half of your shit, twice the money, and you'll do fine.

CHOOSING DESTINATIONS

KEEP YOUR AREAS OF

interest in mind!

Europe has always been the foremost popular destination for backpackers. It's rich in culture, easy to navigate, and has a ton of photo opportunities—and, of course, many sexy Europeans. But, because Europe is not the cheapest destination, you may have to cut your traveling time or spend more time in cheaper countries (Moldova, Romania, Albania, and Bulgaria to name a few) to make up for the difference. To maximize the time you can afford to travel, check out developing areas like Southeast Asia and Central or South America. These places are extremely affordable, generally safe, full of off-track adventures, parties, and hedonistic pleasures.

Questions to ask yourself when planning which country(ies) you want to travel to:

- Beaches or mountains? Need both?
- Sunshine or clouds?
- Cities or countryside?
- English speakers or not?
- Foodie destination or whatever I can eat out of a can?
- Trains (do you need a rail pass?) or planes? Buses or cars?
- Culture (museums, etc.) or outdoors/sports?
- Multiple countries or just one?
- Really safe or a little danger?
- Drink or dry? (If your alcoholic tendencies need to be fed, avoid strict Muslim nations and places where the booze is stupid expensive. Or, use it as an opportunity to detox.)
- Stretch your money or rape your wallet?
- Love festivals/music/concerts or loathe 'em?
- Loads of tourists or tourists are the plague?
- Sex available (free or paid) or fine with Rosie Palm?
- Drugs mandatory or sobriety preferred?

Once you've narrowed down what you need, start looking for places that fit your criteria. Keep these tips in mind when you're chiseling out your itinerary:

- You will most likely plan more activities and destinations than what is realistically possible. Once you start traveling, you'll find that some destinations consume more or less time than what you originally imagined. Remember to check train or bus times between destinations, if that's how you're traveling. The journey between two cities can take an entire day or sometimes more, depending on where you want to go.

- The beauty of backpacking is that you can choose to stay or leave whenever you want. You might even end up traveling with other backpackers you meet along the way. Set up some definite key places to visit and keep other plans flexible.

- You'll be coming across many websites you will want to revisit. Setup a bookmark folder in your browser and save all the websites you find helpful.

- Pinterest.com is a great resource for inspiration to keep track of your favorite destinations.

- As you start planning, you are going to amass a collection of papers, documents, copies, notes, maps, and lots of other things you'll need and might end up losing. As with anything else, you want to be organized from the get-go. We suggest buying a travel journal or planner with inserts to conveniently and securely store this stuff from now until the end of your trip.

- Scan your documents (the ones you don't need to present, like tickets) and keep them in a central file-sharing location, such as Dropbox.com, which has apps for phones and tablets.

CLIMATE AND SEASONS

BETTER WEATHER MEANS you will be competing with bigger crowds and dealing with things being more expensive. Although there could be more action in the midst of tourist madness, it's not a bad idea to hit the "shoulder" seasons, which are just before and just after the "high" season. You'll enjoy cheaper prices, flexible booking arrangements, and a better cultural experience. One small downside is you will likely have to pack for harsher weather. Climates vary dramatically around the world. A good example: Whether it's the rainy season (summer) or the dry season (winter), in some places, the temperature always stays hot or warm. So packing for a winter in Thailand is substantially different than packing for winter in Russia. Also, keep in mind that seasons are opposite above and below the equator—the United States celebrates Christmas when Australia hits the peak of summer. The cherry on top is global warming, which will throw some surprises your way too.

FESTIVALS, HOLIDAYS, AND EVENTS

IF YOU PLAN TO ATTEND any festivals or big events, be sure to make your reservations way in advance (including transportation and accommodations to and from your festival destination). For example, Oktoberfest in Munich attracts a giant tourist crowd (note: it also occurs mostly in September). Tents should be reserved months in advance, as should hostels and couches. Do your research to find what, where, and when things go down. Merchants will often jack up prices of

food and accommodations during festivals, so be sure to budget for the overage. In the Oktoberfest example, hostels are often 300 to 500 percent more expensive during the festival.

LANGUAGE BARRIER

PREPARE FOR SOME SHOCK-ing news. . . . Not everyone in the world speaks English! It's crazy, but it's true. You may actually find yourself in a place where *no one* will speak English. Don't freak out. First off, the best way to learn a language is to immerse yourself in it. You won't have to go out and spend $600 on Rosetta Stone just yet. Although coming to a country speaking a second language will definitely broaden your experience, communicating with people who don't speak your language becomes part of the adventure. Most people will try to help you, but it is essential that you learn the very basics before you go to any country (just to show the locals that you're not arrogant and you're trying). If you're looking to study a new language abroad intensely, Transitions Abroad offers many worldwide language courses and programs. Learn more in our Make Yourself Useful section (page 174).

OTP TIP: Don't carry around a translation book; that's just plain ridiculous. Imagine how you will look whipping out a book when you come up to a stranger and try to ask them about a nearby bar or eatery. Get the Google Translate app instead, for translating more on the down low.

POLITICAL CLIMATE

THE UNITED STATES AND OUR media sometimes embellish the unsafe conditions and extent of political dilemmas present in foreign countries. Be sure to read about the safety conditions and political climates of the countries you plan to visit, but don't be discouraged from visiting destinations the United States advises against. If necessary, take it a step further and do some cross-referencing with the travel advisories of other places like the U.K. and Australia.

Common sense and taking normal precautions will get you by in most places. Wikitravel.com's "Stay Safe" sections are usually written by locals or experienced travelers to that area; it's generally a good site for you to begin to get a valid idea of how dangerous a place really is.

Don't forget, too, that if you're going to a place that has some tensions, political climates can change in an instant. Bone up on the Arab Spring of 2011 for a good read on how governments can sink overnight. Staying on top of foreign events will give you an idea of what to expect. Read the free articles on the *Economist* website, check out Al Jazeera online, and the BBC for news outside the United States.

CULTURE SHOCK

FEELING OVERWHELMED AND

"hating" things, calling an experience or a food "weird," and/or generally wishing you were back home are all pretty telltale signs of culture shock. One of the best ways to avoid it is to get rid of expectations and prep yourself by reading up on the realities of what you'll face. Here are a few of the most common things that can cause people to experience culture shock.

Eats

Nothing can derail a trip faster than a food meltdown. But before you park yourself at McDonalds to chow down on fries in an attempt to shake the shock, read up on the food culture of the country (or countries) you're headed to. You might need to make some dietary concessions, depending on where you are and what the locals serve. Learn ahead of time what the fare might be. If you're a picky eater, have religion-based food restrictions, are vegetarian/vegan, or have a severe food allergy (peanuts would be tough in Thailand or a gluten allergy in Italy), you should plan ahead, knowing what foods you can eat (and the ones you can't), including the names in the local lingo. Also, foods that sound familiar might be completely different—in Spain a tortilla is a potato omelette, not a burrito wrapper or taco shell.

Remember, food is part of the experience. There will be times when you order something and a baked goat head with eyeballs will show up twenty minutes later. Roll with the punches, take a photo for Instagram, and chalk it up to being all part of the journey. It's all going down that culturally shocking shitter anyway.

The Throne

You've been on a hot bus all day long with the windows closed. Everyone is smoking. You're pressed up against a guy with two chickens in his lap. Every bump reminds you that you've needed to pee for the last four hours. You finally stumble out of the bus and find the "bathroom": a plate (that's definitely been used) in the middle of a dirt floor. You cry, and then use it anyway, cursing this godforsaken country. This is a common scenario—from Greece to Turkey to Cambodia to India—and it can cause some serious internal (and external) drama if you're unprepared.

Before you leave the comforts of your home throne (particularly if you're headed to a developing country), figure out the toilet situation in advance. Mental preparation is half the battle in avoiding culture shock.

Guide to Toilets Around the World

SIR THOMAS CRAPPER, ALTHOUGH NOT THE INVENTOR OF the flush-toilet as popularly believed, was a hell of a guy. The pusher of potties, the bad boy of bathrooms, Crapper advocated the use and development of sanitary plumbing for his entire life. The world caught on quickly, and the use of toilets spread globally. Since the humble days of Crapper, people around the world have thought of new and interesting ways to drop off their smellies:

Germany—Poo Platform

Just like a mullet, this shitter is all about business in the front and party in the back. Upon flushing, water rushes out from the back and hypothetically washes your turds into the hole in the front. This interpretation of the toilet is quite counterintuitive, and some major flaws exist with this design. Mainly, the lack of a water barrier between your goods and the toilet creates a horrid preflush smell, and upon flushing, streakage is highly likely.

China—Squatters

These shit holes (very literally) evoke the image of communism. They are bare, rugged, and as it turns out, extremely intimidating to foreigners. There are countless squatter how-to guides that address the important issues, like the fear of falling in. Let's think about this: why are you afraid of a toilet? Here is the only guide you will ever need: see a hole, pull down your pants, squat, and go. ▶

England—The Urilift

The Urilift was invented to remedy the insane amount of drunk-man piss on the streets of England. Whether it fixes the problem or not, this thing kicks ass. During the day, it is hidden in the ground, and when the partying begins, it peeks its smelly head to the surface to service those drunk enough to not care that their bare asses are hanging out in the middle of the street.

Japan—Extreme High Tech

In Japan, your toilet situation is a total crapshoot. On any given visit, you may find yourself hovering over a hole in the ground (see China—Squatters), or at the opposite extreme, you'll have remote-control arm rests that make your stay on the seat very enjoyable and luxurious. Using the high-tech toilet is like flying a space shuttle, with buttons for just about any bathroom predicament you may find yourself in.

There's a noise button to mask the sound of whatever you need to do while in the john (yodeling for instance), one that activates a blow-dryer, a clock to time your visit (handy for when you're training for the logging event in the Bodily Functions Olympics), along with many intricate others.

Russia—Seatless

In one of the coldest places in the world, it's wonderful to know that when you need to go and squatting is not your forte, your ass will probably freeze to the porcelain bowl as no cushy plastic seat is attached. Furthermore, Russians consider toilet paper of any kind a luxury.

Brazil—Button Pushers

Whereas other toilets are preset to flush an average amount of cargo, this one leaves it in your hands. Equipped with a flush button, but no septic tank, your job is to hold the button down for a continual flush until you feel it's time to move on.

Australia—Counterclockwise

Why was the counterclockwise issue ever an issue? Everything will still go down the drain, just in a differently directed spin. What's the problem or the fascination? Who notices these things? You know who—people who stare down at the toilet after they're done. We caught you. We don't care which direction it spins, as long as it goes down.

Sex and Sexes

Depending on where you go, and which gender you happen to be, understand that you might have to bend to cultural norms. If you're a female and covering yourself from head to toe in 110-degree weather sounds like living in a Crock-Pot, avoid Zanzibar during Ramadan. Read up on dress styles and try and pack as close to the local attire as possible. Save a little money for buying appropriate clothing on the road, which will also make great souvenirs when you get back home.

Public displays of affection can get you jailed in some countries, and same-sex overtures can get you beaten or killed in others. Jamaica, for example, has a strong anti-gay culture that has been denounced for years by human rights groups. Don't wait to find out what the sexuality norms are in your destination. Spend some time learning about what's expected of you as a visitor. And, don't forget to pack condoms, birth control, and/or Plan B-types of pills. These might not be readily available, or even legal to buy, where you're headed.

Three Feet of Personal Space

While spending the bulk of an afternoon nuts deep in someone else's chili can be a consensual experience, it's more likely that you're just riding public transportation in a place where personal space is defined a bit differently (which is especially prevalent in many parts of Asia). You'll get to endure hours of odors; you'll know everything that every stranger around you ate for dinner; and you'll smell the sweat of two weeks' worth of sweat that's been baked in the hot sun. Knowing the deal in advance will help you take a deep (mouth open, nose pinched) breath and tell yourself it's all good. Bring a hanky doused in lavender.

Animal Farm

Animals aren't always treated equally, and if animal abuse breaks your heart so much that you can't bear to see it, there are a few places you might want to avoid. Do your due diligence and figure out what's going on with the animal situation where you're going. Understand, too, that what

you feel strongly about probably won't resonate with the locals. Better to be prepared than to be surprised by puppies for sale . . . for dinner.

TRAVEL STYLE: SOLO/PARTNER/GROUP

Solo

IF THIS IS YOUR FIRST TIME

traveling abroad independently, seriously, go solo! We feel damn strongly about this assertion—even if not for the entirety of your trip, at least for a portion. Why? Well, you will decide what *you* want to do, where to go, what you like, dislike, how long to stay, and when to leave. It is a time to learn about *you*! You will have more time to take photos, write in your journal, read, study, observe, and reflect. You will feel empowered to know you can survive on your own with very little in this big world, *freedom at last*! You have the opportunity to meet many other travelers going solo and open yourself up to meeting locals and enriching your cultural experience. For you introverted types, you may find a whole new extroverted you. Traveling solo may sound intimidating at first, but if you overcome the initial hesitation to go solo, the reward will be tenfold. If you are concerned about your safety going solo, check out our Health and Safety section (page 152) to learn how to protect yourself on all fronts.

Travel Partners

If your partner is platonic (and even if he/she isn't), you must closely examine the relationship you have with this person and whether it will withstand the added pressures of traveling. Some things to think about:

- How well do you communicate problems?
- Is your partner independent enough to allow you some alone time?
- Does your partner have his/her own budget/funds?
- Is your partner an experienced traveler?
- Have you spent a prolonged period of time with this person in close quarters before?
- How motivated is your partner to physically travel?
- Does he/she snore? If yes, consider your threshold.
- Is your travel partner really fun at parties? If so, is he/she fun because he/she is drunk and passed out? Maybe you should reconsider.

If you mentally hit on all these points and your partner fails the test, it's probably time to find a new travel partner. Check online for sites that will connect you with like-minded peeps.

But remember, you can always cut out the headache by traveling solo.

Traveling in Groups

You love your friends, so why not have a great time together all around the world? Additionally, traveling en masse might come with the benefits of group rates and split costs. First though, consider the following:

- People smell. One more smell other than your own can be doable; five more smells and you're in nausea territory.
- People bitch. When everyone wants to do the same thing, at the same time, for the same duration, at the same price, traveling in a group is beautiful. Sadly, unless you're all clones of each other, there is no way everyone will always agree on everything. Fights will break out over stupid nonissues and miscommunications.
- People get sick. Some people are whiny when they're sick, and you will have to deal with them dragging you down until they're better.
- People are late. When one person is late, everyone is held up. So enjoying your group rate will be impossible if you miss the flight.
- The bigger the group, the more issues you may have to deal with.

Obviously, it's not impossible to have a great trip as a group, but you will have to compromise your own idea of the perfect trip to incorporate the wants, needs, and quirks of everyone you choose to travel with. If you love your friends more than your sanity, there are several websites that have a good handle on setting up group travel rates at discount prices, such as STA (StaTravel.com).

TECHNOLOGY: THERE'S AN APP FOR THAT

PREPPING FOR YOUR TRIP

isn't just about where to go and what to pack. These days it also includes making sure your technology goes with you. Sure, there are still places on this planet where you'll find yourself in Internet cafés or where the interwebs haven't arrived—and yes, we recommend going there too!—but most of us are digitally dependent. Here are a few apps to download before you hit the road to keep you from getting derailed.

- **Tripadvisor:** There's something to be said for finding restaurants, hotels, and attractions without relentless research, but sometimes you just want someone to tell you if it's infested with cockroaches. Get this app for the heads-up.

- **Hipmunk:** An airline search engine that allows you to filter the search based on more specific variables than just your departure and arrival cities, such as "agony" (i.e., if you're trying to avoid a three-day layover in Jaipur on your way from Frankfurt to Bucharest).

- **Tripit:** Integrates with your calendar and Facebook, and will forward your itinerary to Mom and Dad (or whomever else you want) so they know where you are in space and time.

- **Packing Pro:** For all you list-making types, this will help you keep your shit organized so you won't forget the essentials (like your passport).

- **Postcard Star:** Send your bad-ass photos back home on a postcard. You take a pic; you type your greeting; and then Postcard Star prints and sends it. Bam. Done.

OTP TIP: For accessing those apps on the road (especially the ones that require Wifi) jailbreak your phone so you can buy local sim cards. Want to buy them before you get there? Some locals sell their sims on eBay. Blau.de sells German sims which you can top up anywhere in the world—and Blau gives really great rates outside of Germany as well. LeFrenchMobile.com is dedicated to foreigners traveling in France. Everything is in English, and you can get your own personal French number if you want it. If you're the only one in a group with a local sim and an iPad, be kind to your travel mates—turn your iPad into a Wifi hotspot and let up to five pals tether so they can update Facebook and tend to other "important" digital duties.

RESEARCH: GUIDEBOOKS, BLOGS, AND TRAVEL AGENCIES

GUIDEBOOKS ARE STILL A great source of information for making your travel plans. But with a barrage of travel blogs now all over the Internet, you can find amazing and current insight and advice posted by travel writers who are out traveling your preferred destination right now—so start Googling! Following Twitter feeds of your favorite travelers, expats, and travel sites (@offtrackplanet, in case you were wondering) is also a great way to get inspired and gather intel for your trip.

Guidebooks

Skim through the guides of *Rough Guides*, *Footprint*, *Let's Go*, and *Lonely Planet*, and compare the different publications to see which fits your style best.

- Make sure to check the publication date of the book.
- Unless you intend to spend the majority of your time in one single country, get a book that focuses on an entire continent (or broad region).
- If you do intend to buy books, and you've picked out the ones you like, buy them online! You can save up to 85 percent buying used books through Amazon or Half.com.

- Instead of bringing your massive guidebook (which will occupy prime real estate in your backpack and make you look like a douche), tear out the pages you need, staple them together, and stick it in your travel journal.
- You can only afford to buy one guidebook? No prob. You can always go to your local library, as they carry recent releases of most guidebooks. Check them out and write down or type up what you need.
- Don't forget the apps. These days, a lot of travel guides have free or cheap apps for your country of choice.

TRAVEL AGENTS AND TOUR GUIDES

Travel Agents

These guys take the discount hunting for your travel needs out of your hands. In many countries, taking a GAP year (a year off to travel before moving on to college or work) is popular, and some travel agencies cater specifically to the GAP-year crowd. Using these guys can result in some killer deals for eighteen- to twenty-five-year-olds.

The United Kingdom (a GAP-year country) has some good sites, so include "U.K." as a keyword in your searches. Unfortunately, travel agencies in the United States generally cater to an older, less "backpacky" traveling crowd. (Yes, we think this sucks too . . . we're working on it.) For the most part, agents will try to sell you prepackaged guide tours, which are boring and a cop-out to real backpacking. One agency that comes close to understanding the needs of backpackers is STA Travel, who generally caters to young people twenty-five and under.

Tour Guide Packages

Packaged tour guides provide you with a choice of itineraries that are full of popular travel destinations and activities. You'll have a built-in group of travel companions, and you won't have to worry about the details. This might be the right decision for some, but this also *defeats the purpose of independent travel*. It's touristy as hell, and, just like your trip, your travel stories will be bland and prepackaged. But, if you're into that kind of thing, check out Intrepid Travel and Contiki.

Finally, don't stress out too much about trying to figure everything out all at once. One of the most valuable things you'll learn from this experience is how adaptable you are. In fact, you might even miss the point if you stay completely within all your plans. This is a journey enhanced by learning to change direction or by getting a bit . . . fuck it, for the sake of being cheesy, *off track*!

PASSPORTS
and VISAS

IN ORDER TO LEAVE THIS COUNTRY, YOU'LL NEED A PASSPORT.
Some countries also require visas for entrance or to work, study, or stick around a while. This is step one to get you off your ass and into the world. We've been there and have the rashes to prove it, so here is what you need to get started.

TRAVEL.STATE.GOV

THIS U.S. DEPARTMENT OF State website is something our government has actually done right. It has well-organized, complete, and official information regarding passports, visas, embassies, and guidelines for visiting every country on the planet. You should visit this website early and often when planning any international trip.

PASSPORT

YOUR TICKET TO THE WORLD, any U.S. citizen can get a passport. Here's how:

1. Dig up your proof of citizenship (birth certificate, previous passport, or certificate of citizenship) and grab a driver's license or state ID.

2. Make a copy, front and back, of both forms of ID.

3. Get one passport picture at any drugstore with a photo department in five minutes for about $10. Take off your glasses; don't wear a hat or bling; and don't smile. No kissy faces, and keep your shirt on.

4. Go to Travel.state.gov/passport/ and fill out the DS-11 form online. Print it out.

5. Submit your application at a post office or municipal government office.

Routine processing for a passport takes four to six weeks and costs $110 (plus $25 for first-timers). Expedited processing is two to four weeks and will run you an extra $60. If you're traveling within two weeks or need to get a visa within four, it will cost extra, but you can schedule an appointment at one of the twenty-five government passport agencies, and they'll hook you up with a little blue book faster.

PASSPORT CARD

A PASSPORT CARD CAN BE used to travel to Mexico, Canada, or the Caribbean by land or sea (not air!). The application process is about the same as for a passport book, but it fits in your wallet and is $80 cheaper. It's handy if you live near a border and cross it often, but for the type of travel you should be doing, you'll need a passport book.

How to Handle Your Passport

Don't lose it! Take plenty of precautions. Don't walk around with your passport (unless the country you're in requires you to have it at all times). Instead, carry a copy of your passport and visa (if there is one) in your wallet, stash one in your bag, and give one to a travel buddy. Also, e-mail a copy of your passport and visas to

Who's Your Daddy? What the U.S Embassy Can Do for You

Who Are These Guys?

A U.S. embassy is the headquarters for U.S. affairs in a foreign country and assists and protects the rights of Americans in that country. Embassies are in most foreign capital cities, and consulates (basically a junior embassy) are in many other major cities. Both are there to help you when you're screwed.

The STEP Program

Relax, we're not sending you to rehab (yet). The STEP Program is provided for free by the government to assist you abroad in case of an emergency and to send you routine info or travel advisories from certain embassies. It takes just a few minutes to set up an account at Step.state.gov and register your upcoming trips. So do it.

What the U.S. Embassy Can Do

If you lose your passport, the embassy will whip you up an emergency one in no time. If you need medical help, they can direct you to some good local docs or help arrange a return to the states, if needed. If you get robbed, they can tell you where to file a police report and help you get money from home if you lose everything. If you're completely SOL, they may even give you a loan to get back to the states. Broken heart? Deal with it, you sissy.

What the U.S. Embassy Can't Do

If you fuck up and get thrown in some dingy foreign slammer, the U.S. embassy will not send in SEAL Team Six to whisk you away to safety. You're expected to abide by the laws of the country you are in, even if those laws are different than back home. So if you get busted committing international atrocities such as gum-chewing in Singapore or PDA in Dubai, don't expect Uncle Sam to bail you out.

What If I Am Arrested?

You may not get your one phone call, but foreign law enforcement should let you contact your embassy, which can point you to a local lawyer, contact your one cool uncle for bail money, and make sure you are treated humanely according to international law. Unless you indicate otherwise, the embassy must legally keep any info about you private, so Mommy never has to know you were trying to pick up a tranny hooker.

When Shit Really Hits the Fan

If a military coup is threatening to disrupt your hammock time, make sure you are registered with the local embassy through STEP and follow the suggestions in e-mails or news reports. If shit gets bad, they may recommend you leave the country. If shit gets *really* bad and commercial travel isn't safe, they may even coordinate an evacuation.

yourself in case you lose all your shit and need to prove to Uncle Sam at an embassy that you are family.

If you *do* lose it . . . U.S. passports let you move rather easily around most of the world (good news), so the black market for them is huge (bad news). If it gets lost or stolen, go to the nearest U.S. embassy. They will wipe your tears and get you a replacement ASAP.

VISAS

A VISA IS A DOCUMENT OR

stamp placed in your passport that acts as an endorsement to enter a country. Many countries require a visa for entrance, and most do for work, study, or extended stays. Some you can get at the border (or when you arrive), and others you need to obtain in advance. Specifications and requirements can vary widely—for most places in Europe you don't even need one. If you're looking for a visa to trek around places not in the EU, however, you'll need to take a look at their visa requirements. Once again, Travel.state.gov will let you know all the specifics for entering a country, as well as where to go to get a visa, if needed. Plan ahead—some visas take weeks to get, and sometimes if you don't have one, you'll be denied boarding on your flight or will be turned away at the border.

MONEY *and* BUDGETING

BEFORE YOU START PLANNING YOUR BUDGET, YOU SHOULD have a little convo with yourself about what the word "budget" actually means to you. Staying true to broke-ass backpacker ideals by always choosing the cheapest option may take its toll after several months of sleeping on the ground for free and eating $2 street-meat. As such, factoring in a little cash to treat yourself to a nice room and a sit-down meal may be something to think about. Keepin' it real with yourself about how low you're willing to go is essential in determining how much money you'll need once you get to your destination.

PRE-TRIP EXPENSES (ALL PRICES USD)

Backpack: $120 to $300

Besides plane tickets, your backpack can be the most expensive purchase of the entire trip. Make sure to try on a bunch and do some comparative shopping before you say "I do" to the one you love. A backpack with a day-pack can be worth the extra money. And, do yourself a favor: spend a few extra bucks on a lock—at the very least, it's $10 well-spent to protect your big travel investment.

Travel Supplies/ Toiletries: $30 to $100

Although keeping your dirty parts clean is key, you don't need a bunch of eau-de-what-not products to do so. Buy a few basic travel-size items to get you started and remember that people all over the world get by just fine without $25 shampoo. Bringing a few items like aspirin and anti-diarrhea tablets along could be a lifesaver if you get the runs on the road and don't know where the local drugstore is.

Vaccinations: $0 to $300

You don't want your trip cut short by an incurable disease. So, once you decide where you want to go, check out the Centers for Disease Control website at Cdc.gov. Click on your destination country (or countries), and you'll find a list detailing all diseases present in that region and the vaccinations you'll need to get. Call around to several travel clinics and doctors to see whose stab rates are the lowest—and it's worth asking if you can bargain a price for a one-stop-shot. Don't put off getting stabbed until the last minute: some vaccines take up to eight weeks to start working their magic.

Passport/Visa Fees: $0 to $250

Passports and visas are costs you cannot avoid. Certain countries require their own special visa, so factor that cost in, as well. You won't get very far across any border without a passport; so make sure that *all* of your documents are up to date. Make copies of and scan, then e-mail yourself all important papers before you leave.

Discount Cards: $22 to $28

If you're a full-time student, buying an International Student Identity Card (ISIC) could save you much more than the price of the card itself (around $22). Having one of these cards gets you discounts on a variety of things, from museums to train tickets. If you're not a student and under 26, you can apply for an International Youth Travel Card (IYTC), which gets you all the same benefits as the ISIC. For $28 you can become a member of Hostelling International and get discounts on hostel bookings, museum admissions, and travel services.

Travel Insurance: $60 to $260

We get why some people would skip travel insurance to save a few bucks, but unless you plan on traveling in a bubble while wearing a padded suit, consider travel insurance a priority if you're visiting slightly sketchy places. The fact is that you never know what could happen—and while we're not trying to be your mother, we doubt you have an extra $10,000 to $100,000 lying around in case a major medical emergency happens. Travel insurance will also cover bag loss (or theft), and offers 24/7 phone support if the shit hits the fan.

Transportation: $300 to $5,000

There are more websites to help you find cheap flights than there are airlines. But, remember to read the fine print of ticketing restrictions before you click "buy"—some sites will charge you a booking fee that can be avoided by going to the airline website directly. Factoring in all the costs of planes, trains, and automobiles can be tricky, so plan on overestimating just in case you want to splurge on a cab back to the hostel. Some hostels rent bikes for minimal fees, and nothing beats the price of walking.

ON THE ROAD

BEFORE YOU HIT THE ROAD,
make sure to find out the current exchange rate for the country you are visiting. We recommend consulting Xe.com when gauging how far you can stretch your dollar.

Accommodations: $0 to $60 per night

Consider hostels your new home away from home while traveling. Cheaper than even the most budget-friendly hotels, most hostels will sleep anywhere from two to twenty in a room (private rooms are available in most for more money) and will offer some of the best opportunities for meeting like-minded travelers, or hot, temporary bed-mates. Depending on where you are traveling, the time of year, and exchange rates, the price of hostels can vary significantly. If paying $5 for a bed seems like too much, check out Couchsurfing.org.

Eating/Drinking: $5 to $20 per day

In general, this is a cost that varies according to how much you like to eat, how restrictive your dietary needs are, and how many drinks it takes you to get a sufficient buzz. In many countries, eatin' on the streets is the most authentic and least expensive way to grub. Finding a hostel with a kitchen can be a win-win situation that saves you cash and

scores you ass. Everyone knows that the fastest way to any hottie's heart is through the stomach, so hit up the local market for some groceries and whip up a cheap meal that will impress the traveling tail.

Sightseeing/ Museums: $0 to $100 per week

While your nights may be filled with bars and clubs, your days will likely be filled with cultural activities. Decide which sights you are willing to pay to see and for which just snapping a pic and moving on will suffice. Staring at the Eiffel Tower from afar is free, while getting to the top will cost ya. Most museums will have one day of the month when they are free for all, so it's worth doing a little investigating before you plunk down a wad of cash on admission fees. Many museums will offer student discounts, while others will suggest a donation. With so much shit to see in every country, fees can add up quickly—skip some of the touristy places with pricey admissions in favor of smaller attractions—everyone visits the Louvre in Paris, but how many can say they've been to Le Musée des Vampires? Check out the first section

of this book for quirky inspiration (page 10).

Partying: $10 to $50 per week

Get your party started right by doing some pre-gamin' in the hostel. You can split the cost of a bottle with your hostel mates and play some international drinking games before heading out to save some in-bar cash. Many hostels will have their own bar with cheap drink specials— and the added bonus of being close to your bed for those moments when you meet a "special friend."

Communicating: $5 per week

Outside of checking in with Moms and Pops to let them know how responsible you're being (wink, wink), this is one cost that can be kept to a bare minimum. You didn't travel across the world to be on the phone, so let people know you're alive with a quick e-mail from a cheap Internet café. If you're dying to see the boyfriend you left behind, get some face-time for free via Skype. Or, you can also purchase an international calling card upon arrival. Remember that you can tell everyone about your trip for free when you get back.

Laundry: $2 to $10 per week

Many hostels will have laundry facilities on-site for a small fee. If not, ask the front desk where the nearest coin-operated Laundromat is. Otherwise, buy a small box of detergent and make a sink your new washing machine—use your bedposts as an overnight air-dryer and you'll have a nice, clean pair of skivvies by the morning. The straps on your back-pack also make a great dryer when times get rough. If you're on foot and it's warm out, loop a few things through your straps to give them some fresh-air time.

Souvenirs: $5 to $25

Bringing back a trinket from your trip can be a nice gesture to say, "I was somewhere cooler than you were." Steer clear of the tourist shops that will jack up all the prices on lame, touristy crap that no one wants. Instead, check out local flea markets or artist fairs to score one-of-a-kind tchotchkes on the cheap. Saving your shopping until the last day or two will save you from hauling other people's shit all over the world with you.

Miscellaneous: $20 per week

You want to have a little cushion money for things that may pop up that aren't necessarily essential expenses. For times when you find out about a concert or festival you're psyched about while on the road, you unexpectedly run out of shampoo because the chick you're hooking up with used it to wash her lion mane, you feel like tricking out your back-pack with hydraulics, or whatever it may be, having a bit of extra spend-ing money not reserved for anything in particular is nice. Just don't con-sider this a spike to your drinking budget, or you'll end up in the gutter, penniless.

BACKPACKS
and PACKING

ONCE YOU'RE OUT AND ABOUT, YOU'LL BE SURPRISED AT
how little you actually need. The less you bring, the more resourceful
you'll learn to be.

CHOOSING YOUR BACKPACK

YOUR PACK WILL BE ON

your back like a nagging wife whom you can't divorce any time soon. Do not buy a pack online without first giving it an in-person test run. Price is important when picking your pack, but so are your frame size, shape, and determining just how many of those buckles and zippers you need. Employees with experience under their hip straps can suit you up properly. You're looking for something that distributes weight evenly, so don't be afraid to throw some weights in the pack and walk around the store to test it. This is when you ask a lot of questions without worrying about looking or sounding stupid. Once you've found the chosen one, compare prices online and see if you can get a better deal at a different store or online. Local retailers will sometimes match online prices.

PACKING

THIS AIN'T NO WEEKEND

trip: procrastination packing will leave you in the middle of a shitstorm without a raincoat. Think about the climate you'll be hitting, the weather patterns in the regions you visit, and the duration of your trip. To maximize space, use the roll method. Military-style packing conserves a surprising amount of space and saves you from the dorky crease lines

OTP TIPS

- Bigger isn't always better. A 50- to 65-liter pack (about 20 to 30 pounds when stuffed) should do the trick.

- The weight of your world will be on your shoulders and hips—make sure both shoulder and hip straps are padded. Hip straps can take 40 percent of the weight off your shoulders.

- Everybody loves easy access. A zip-front opening is crucial so that getting to your clean underwear isn't a twenty-minute mission.

- Daypacks are super useful. There will be plenty of days when you'll leave your pack at the hostel and want a small backpack for exploration. Some packs come with a daypack built in, but if yours doesn't, choose a regular old backpack that you can wear on your front with your bigger pack on your back.

- Keep all that important shit—passport, medicines, camera—in your daypack and guard it like a pit bull.

- Looks really don't matter. You're going to abuse the snot out of this thing. It'll be sat on, used as a pillow, crammed in dirty storage spaces and under buses, and hell, with all those straps, you can even use it as a drying rack for your wet clothes. Stitch on some patches if you're looking for style.

made by folding clothes suitcase-style. Some travelers opt for space-saving bags, which compress clothes and other items in airtight compartments. Medium-size, water-proof stuff sacks are great for organizing too, and can come in handy whenever things get moist.

Clothing

No matter which small, dusty, unde-veloped corner of the world you're going to, you don't need as much shit as you think. Fashionistas can pull it off with minimal clothes, and you'll want some room in your pack for on-the-road finds. Pack with sac-rifice in mind—if you're not sure that you'll need it, you probably don't. You should bring enough clothes to last about two weeks without having to do laundry. A little dirt is part of the backpacker ethos, but leave the whites at home to be more discreetly filthy.

Don't max out your credit card for "traveler wear"—you'd feel like a nerd in zip-off lightweight khakis anyway. Pack two or three pairs of pants you feel comfortable in, both on the dance floor and on the trail. Ladies can replace one pair of pants with an ankle-length skirt for variety. Ankle-length is ideal because you won't trip on it while hauling ass, no one will mistake you for a streetwalker, and it can oftentimes double as a tube dress or long top.

Three or four T-shirts will do the trick. When you're ready for a change, bust out the scissors and turn your T-shirts into tank tops. Two or three good pairs of sweat-

resistant, made-for-walkin' socks will suffice, and three to five pairs of underwear will be fine if you wash them regularly.

Don't take more than three pairs of shoes. You'll want either running shoes or hiking boots, shoes for wan-dering around or going out, and a pair of flip flops. Many hostels have shared showers where foot grossities are waiting to take your little piggies to nastyland, and having the flip flops will save you from fungus.

No matter what weather you're headed into, the importance of a good, lightweight raincoat can't be overstated. Marmot makes a super-snazz one that folds up into its own pocket. Aside from obvious uses, when you couple this puppy with a fleece or a hoodie, you've got your northernmost face covered. Layering is key.

If you're planning on being in win-tery climes or high altitudes, pack a good wool hat and scarf, waterproof gloves, and long underwear. Colum-bia makes some new-fangled long johns that are both sweat-resistant and heat-trapping, and for high-altitude trekking, the investment is worthwhile. Remember, though, you can always stock up on shit when you need it. If you're going somewhere where the dollar is still strong, buying stuff like hats and scarves beats lugging them around.

Sleep Gear

You'll spend about a third of your trip sleeping, so packing stuff to make downtime comfortable is important. Overnight buses and trains don't come with pillows, and at particularly grungy hostels, it's nicer to sleep on your own drool stains than somebody else's. You'll want a small pillow, preferably an inflatable one that folds up. A sleeping sack can be made for free by sewing up two sides of an old folded sheet—a great, lightweight addition to your pack that allows you to avoid contact with others' bodily fluids. A pack of lightweight earplugs is worthwhile if you're not so into night noises.

Bathroom Essentials

Not overpacking toiletries is the easiest way to save on space and weight. Plan on buying extra shampoo and deodorant on the road, even if you can't find your favorite brand. A travel towel made from lightweight, quick-drying material is a must. Sunscreen and bug spray are good to grab before you go; the cost of sunscreen can burn if locals don't use it. Ladies: bring at least a couple weeks' worth of Aunt Flo's favorites in case you can't find them when you need them. And no

one should be without at least a few condoms, even if you're not planning on getting busy—you never know. Don't forget your toothbrush.

First Aid

You may not be an EMT, but it's worth packing a few essentials like Band-Aids, antibacterial cream, and Steri-Strips (for instantly binding bad cuts) to play it safe. Pharmacies abroad are different than they are at home. While you can sometimes get just about any drug you want—including Valium and Oxy—it can be difficult to find the simple stuff like aspirin or allergy pills. Make sure all of your necessary prescriptions are clearly labeled and you have enough for the duration of your trip. Pack a small bottle of headache medicine (for those nasty hangovers) and something to handle a bad cold. Tap water is a no-no in almost all developing countries. If you're planning on roughing it, bring at least a few water purification tablets—drinking funky water will definitely slow you down and spoil your trip.

Safety Gear

You will need a lock to safely leave your backpack in the hostel locker. An old-fashioned Masterlock will work for some places, but since locker hole sizes vary widely, a lock with a thinner loop is a better bet. If you're into super-safety, you might be interested in Pacsafe's stainless-steel locking net device to cover your pack. Packing a money belt depends on how paranoid/much of a nerd you are.

Tech Gear

A camera is a must, and it's a good idea to pack an extra SD card, an extra camera battery, and a USB cable to load your photos onto Facebook at Internet cafés. Even if you're not the writer type, chances are you'll want a journal and a couple pens. A loaded mp3 player is a lifesaver, and if yours doesn't have a reliable alarm, you'll need to pack a small travel alarm clock. This becomes necessary when train and bus schedules dictate exact wake-up times. Keep pricey gadgets to a minimum. If you can't easily replace it, don't bother bringing it. Everything else will be available on the road. If not, you will figure out how to either make do without it or whine until someone forks over their stash of whatever it is you forgot.

FLIGHTS *and* TRANSPORTATION

BUYING THAT INITIAL PLANE TICKET OUT OF THE COUNTRY can be hard on the wallet. Ticket prices vary widely from one continent to the next and within regions. A ticket to Paris is sometimes comparable in cost to a semester's tuition, but a flight from Paris to London can run you the price of a pack of Wrigley's (as in less than one euro; shocking but true). Here's the rundown on getting from point A to point B, with a bunch of sea in between.

BLAST OFF

START YOUR TRIP FROM THE

cheapest location in the United States possible. If you live in Bumble-fuck, you're likely to save big by arranging transportation to a major international hub. This could mean volunteering to drive an old lady's car to Florida, taking a Greyhound to New York, or hopping a train to Houston, Chicago, or Dallas. Amtrak, Greyhound, Megabus, and car exchanges are surprisingly cheap ways to get around the States.

When booking from the big city, expand your horizons. While sites like Priceline and Travelocity have the best commercials, check out other sites like Momondo.com, which compares several airlines and dates at once so that you can get a general idea of ticket prices. Keeping your dates flexible sets you up for finding the best rates possible. Smaller airlines often have crazy-good deals on their official sites, as well—Spirit Air, for example,

sometimes offers flights for under $100 from Miami to Bogota, Colombia. STA Travel is an old-school travel agency that has sixteen locations around the country, all close to college campuses. With a student ID, you can score a ticket at a price that will make businessmen jealous.

If you're heading out to do some good in the world, there are organizations that subsidize transportation. If you're set up to volunteer, check out FlyForGood.com and score a discount on airfare to the volunteer destination. Flip through our Make Yourself Useful section (page 174) to get some ideas on how to go the good route.

Getting off-grid is great, but keeping that smartphone active could be helpful. There are a ton of apps that make travel smoother. FlightStats specializes in tracking flights, and Gate-Guru provides useful maps of sprawling international hubs. Delta has an app to track your luggage, which is helpful when everything you own is at the mercy of multiple airports.

TYPES OF TICKETS

FLIGHTS DON'T JUST COME and go. There are several different types of airline tickets—some with more tricks up their sleeve than Amelia Earhart.

Round-Trip

If you only have a short time, or if you're Captain Organized and have your route planned out, opt for a tried-and-true round-trip ticket. Choose a spot to bookend your travels, and plan to use local or regional transportation between destinations. A round-trip ticket can be reassuring, especially for travel virgins, because beginning and end dates are tangible. It can also be cheaper in the long run: a single-leg ticket to London, for example, is sometimes only slightly less than a round-trip one. Just keep in mind that once you do this, you're locked in.

Go and Don't Come Back

If you've got more time on your hands or don't know exactly where you want to go, join the ranks of bank robbers and fugitives and book a seat one-way. With a one-way ticket, you're as flexible as a yoga teacher. Say you're chilling with a group in Tangiers that's headed to Dubai tomorrow, and you decide you want to tag along. No set plans for a return trip home? Score. Those palm-shaped islands are yours. Just be sure to set aside enough in your bank account to get home eventually—unless you're planning on pulling a Bonnie and Clyde.

Open-Jaws

These are multidestination tickets that make your trip a three-way. You'll still pick a place to bookend your travels, but you can also hit up a couple of spots in between. An open-jaw ticket typically goes from Point A to B to C and back to A. You'd be interested in one of these if you're trying to cover mad ground, or if long-distance trains and buses aren't your thing. They're also good if you're planning to travel for six months or more, because it gives your wandering a backbone and keeps aimless vagabonding tendencies in check.

Airpasses

Airpasses are promotional packages offered by allied airlines around the world. Each pass has a predetermined list of cities you can choose from, and the ticket price includes a stop in each city you choose. Residents of any city included are ineligible for an Airpass. You're sacrificing flexibility, but if you score a good deal, you can always tack on more time before or after your set itinerary.

Around the World (RTW)

An RTW ticket is like buying whole-sale—each ticket included costs a little bit less than it would alone. Beginning at roughly $3,000, an RTW can be a lot to put out, but other than trying to paddle a raft around the globe for forty years, this is the cheapest way to see the world. Do your research: some include party fouls such as only being able to fly in one direction or having to book round-trips. Check out OneWorld.com, SkyTeam.com, and StarAlliance.com to get started.

MILE HIGH CLUB

Join the Mile-High Club!

JUST GETTING LAID WON'T get you many high fives anymore. To join the truly elite lovers club, board a plane and engage in some freaky activity 40,000 feet above the ground. Here's how:

GET A PARTNER

Unless you're with someone you hump regularly, you'll need to scout out a partner. Don't be a boarding gate creeper, but hit up the nearest airport pub instead. Scan the bar for a boarding pass with the same flight, "randomly" grab a seat next to your target and get to work.

TIMING

Timing is key. On overnight flights, wait until everyone is asleep or watching Nicolas Cage ruin a movie. On shorter flights, wait for the drink service to start. The flight attendants are your mile-high cock blocks, so make sure they are distracted.

MAKE YOUR MOVE

Do your prep work at the seat and go *one at a time* to a predetermined bathroom. On the bigger overnight planes, the mid-cabin bathrooms are bigger, and flight attendants linger in the back all night. On daytime flights, the back bathrooms are your love lavs—out of sight from the rest of the cabin.

THE ACT

You're not here to set any marathon records, so no need to think of sports to prolong this one. Get in, and get out. Bring a rubber—you won't find condom dispensers in these bath-rooms. When you're done, walk to your seats separately and avoid eye contact. Either way, the deed is done, and no amount of shame can take away your membership card.

Congratulations to the newest inductees of the mile-high club. It's about time you stopped flying *Virgin*.

ONCE YOU'RE THERE

WHILE OUR HIGHWAYS KICK
ass and the road trip is as American as apple pie, we're behind the times when it comes to getting around on the ground. Most parts of the world have elaborate train and bus systems that make Amtrak look like your toy set around the Christmas tree, and Greyhound look like a Chihuahua. There's no better way to understand the true essence of a country than by utilizing its mass-transit systems, and in most backpacker hot spots, mass transit is the fastest and most reliable way to get around.

Eurail Passes

European train trips are legendary—chances are if you've been to Europe, you've boarded one of these bad boys. Travel between European countries is more like crossing a state line, and the über-developed train system is your ticket to just about anywhere. If you're backpacking across Europe for a while, your best bet is to buy a Eurail Pass.

Broken down by distance of travel, there are several different types of passes. The Global Pass includes all rail travel to and within twenty-three countries. A Select Pass gives you access to between three and five countries, and a Regional Pass enables you to travel within and

between two different countries. If you're planning on spending your whole sojourn getting spiritual with Greek goddesses or exercising your Italian stallion for a while, opt for a One Country Pass, where travel is unlimited within the country of choice. Tickets are cheaper the younger you are—snag a youth ticket for a 35 percent discount. If both you and your travel partner are twenty-six or older, the Small Group Saver will knock off 15 percent. There are a handful of Eurail apps that will bring train schedules to your fingertips, which can make all the difference in the world.

Asian Trains

Getting around China or India by car or bus ain't no European holiday. Heavy road traffic is caused by animals with the same right-of-way as rickshaws and enough people to clog the world's arteries. Metal bus seats and bumpy roads can leave your ass baboon blue after a long trip. The best way to get around these giant countries is to train it. There are several different class levels, and they vary from country to country.

Train compartments hold up to six people, and overnight trains usually have a Sleeper Class. Opt for a top bunk if you're into personal space, because lower berths serve as benches during the daytime. A cramped General Class ticket is hardly worth the money you'll save. Most trains also have a more expensive AC Sleeper Class, in which you'll find more privacy and less sweat.

Busabout

Busabout, which operates throughout nine countries in Europe (with routes in Northern Africa), is comparable to Eurorail in the way that it works. You'll be issued a pass based on your preferred destinations and length of travel. Busabout tickets, however, are specifically designed for backpackers, so bust out that booze and make some friends. There are adventure, trekking, festival-geared, and hop-on, hop-off options. Check out Busabout.com to create your own trip.

South American Buses

Nowhere in the world is there a more developed bus system than the international routes crisscrossing South America. The quality of these buses depends on the wealth of your country of origin. Long-distance Argentine buses, for example, are usually double-decker, air-conditioned beauties with fully reclining seats and even free hot coffee. Buses in Bolivia or Ecuador are a lot rougher, but they've got character—and build it, too.

International pricing varies from country to country, but it's almost always cheaper than flying. You'll need to budget for Colombian buses, but the bus route running the gringo trail from La Paz to Cusco will hardly dent your wallet. Be sure to hit up the terminal ticket booth a day before you want to travel, and don't forget to ask if the bus has a bathroom on board.

Reinventing the Road Trip

Rental cars are usually the most expensive mode of transport, but there's nothing quite like getting behind the wheel, rolling down the windows, blasting some good tunes, and conquering foreign roads. You'll find an agency in any major airport— Avis, Budget, Europcar, Hertz, and Thrifty are all international companies. Some have apps to save you long-ass lines at the airport and frustrating miscommunication. Not every country requires an International Driving Permit, but some do. You can get one at your local DMV before leaving. Keep in mind that road signs will be in the language of the country and you'll have to figure out which side of the road to drive on. Be prepared to be confused while in motion.

The World's Most Skateable Cities

SKATEBOARDING, NOW THE world's grittiest sponsorship sport, started in the 1940's when the waves weren't gnarly enough for California surfers. Street surfing hit the scene rolling, and in 1964 the first international skateboarding championship was held in Anaheim. Once liability suits threatened to keep skaters off the streets, skate parks popped up from Florida to Tokyo. Kickflip the shit out of these awesome international skate parks:

- At **Amazing Square Skatepark,** smack in the middle of Tokyo, you can skate the core of a major metropolis without a police baton up your ass. In addition to some hardcore street courses, Amazing Square has plenty of verticals and a giant half-pipe.

- You a bowl lover? At **Bondi Beach Skatepark,** just outside of Sydney, a killer view is a bonus to catching some air in the epic bowls. All the bikinis aren't a bad deal, either.

- There's a ton of class-act skateparks in France, but **Marseille Skatepark** is top dog. Grind up in this trippily graffitied course for free, and take a dip in the Mediterranean at the beach next door to wash off the skate sweat.

- The **SMP Skatepark** in Shanghai, China, is a cultural revolution, with 45,000 square feet of rails, stairs, bowls, ramps, and a viewing plaza to watch the action.

- If you're hard enough to flip it old-school, hit up the **Livingston Skatepark** in Livingston, Scotland. This skull-lined bowl is legendary.

- Leave it to the guys who started it all to come up with the mother of all skateparks—California's **Lake Cunningham Regional Skatepark** in San Jose boasts a 70-by-22-foot full pipe, massive bowls, pools, a mega wall, and a street course. Bring some Band-Aids.

HEALTH and SAFETY

GLOBE-TROTTING IS SAFER THAN YOU THINK, AND ARMING yourself with awareness is your best defense against any bug or thug abroad. You can't protect yourself from every incident, but you can take precautions that will help keep your trip on track and worry-free. Using common sense, washing your hands, and being aware of your surroundings goes a long way. Here are more specific things we have learned on the road.

IMMUNIZATIONS, DISEASE, AND PARASITES

GENERALLY, PLACES THAT are least developed are most prone to disease; tropical areas have some nasty bugs (like worms that swim into your pisser), and the world water supply isn't always microbe-free. As a liability catchall, certain areas in the world have been flagged by the United States as "no-go" health zones to deter Americans from traveling there, but that doesn't mean they're actually impossible (or super dangerous) to explore. As long as you have the proper gear and knowledge, there's no need to let the fearmongers stop you from going anywhere in the world.

Shoot Up Before You Head Out

Depending on where you're headed, you might need to be inoculated against parasites or diseases, particularly in developing countries. To find out which vaccinations are required to visit any country, go to the Centers for Disease Control (CDC) website: Cdc.gov. If you want a second opinion, check out the British Foreign & Commonwealth Office (Fco.gov.uk) for their vaccination suggestions, as well.

Water Is Important, but Beware

Water with microscopic nasties can turn your globe-trotting into a trip to the crapper. Unless you like impromptu colonics, we suggest you stick to bottled water and avoid ice cubes in drinks. Just drinking booze the entire time will help you avoid the bugs, but might not be so great for staying hydrated (or avoiding cirrhosis). The water in most places in Europe is generally safe, but no matter where you go, read up on what the water situation is for that country.

Health Care Varies

You might be surprised at the quality of health care available in many places and horrified at others. Some medicines that require prescriptions in the United States are over-the-counter abroad and vice versa. (For instance, topical steroids such as cortizone often need a prescription in other countries, but you can stock up on Viagra without a doctor's note.) There are some areas where meds are hard to come by, so coming prepared with common travel antibiotics and a decent first-aid kit in hand will serve you well. Having some rubbers with you never hurts (unless that's what you're into).

Read Up on What the Locals Know

Following Twitter feeds, reading blogs, and checking out expat forums are all good ways to find out critical information on staying disease-free during your travels. For example, in certain areas you'll want to iron your underwear . . . seriously. When traveling around the sub-Saharan tropics (and some parts of tropical Central and South America), ironing all of your clothes (including your dainties) will kill eggs from the Putzi (or Tumbo) fly, which burrows into your skin. Finding out the scoop from people who live in these areas will give you a heads-up on the realities of what's safe and what isn't.

TRAVEL CLINICS

TRAVEL CLINICS ARE THE ZEN masters of getting you inoculated against the world of internal creepy-crawlies. These are places where doctors specifically see patients who will be traveling, particularly to developing countries, and are a great resource for both getting you in good health before your trip, as well as hooking you up with info to keep you healthy while abroad. Find your local travel clinic and chat with the doctor about eight weeks before your trip, as some immunizations and meds need time to kick in. If you have insurance, check to see what is covered.

The medical staff will have a lot of questions to ask you about your travels, so try to get at least some of your plans straightened out before you give them a visit. Focus on figuring out which countries you will hit and for how long (the length of your stay sometimes dictates your level of risk and changes the vaccines you may need). Read up on the immunizations suggested for your specific country on the CDC website (Cdc.gov) and make sure you let the doc know

about all your current ailments. Once all of your preventative measures are in order, talk to your doctor about getting antibiotics for the road. Fill all your current prescriptions with extras to cover the time you're traveling (remember the liquid carry-on limitations for things like liquid meds and saline solution). You may need to start some regimens (i.e., malaria pills) a few days before you depart. Keep copies of your immunization records with you during your trip.

FIRST AID AND MEDICATIONS

WHILE MOST COUNTRIES have well-stocked local pharmacies, it can be a pain trying to find what you want or need, particularly when there is a language barrier and especially if you're not feeling your best. Here are a few of the essentials to take with you for quick fixes on the go.

Over-the-Counter Essentials

You can MacGyver yourself into relatively good health using the following list of items. For the heavier stuff, always bring your original prescription in case there's a dispute at the border—but things like diabetic insulin, birth control, allergy, and asthma inhalers should be fine.

- Antibacterial hand sanitizer
- Ibuprofen, acetaminophen, and/or naproxen
- Sunscreen
- Chapstick
- Bug spray
- Band-Aids/blister plasters like Compeed
- Neosporin
- Imodium A-D/Pepto
- Preparation H
- Sleeping/anxiety pills
- Condoms
- Thermometer
- Anti-nausea/motion-sickness pills
- Aloe or lidocaine

FOOD

AS WITH WATER, FOOD

around the world contains different things that can shoot through you faster than a hot knife through butter. It's not a pretty thought, but it's worse to be unprepared when you feel the familiar (and painful) gut gurgling begin. Besides the obvious, prolonged diarrhea can cause dehydration, malnutrition, and major discomfort. Still, treat yourself to authentic food joints, but remember, your body needs time to acclimate to all of the new foods you're shoveling in. Give your innards some time to build up the necessary good microbes to digest these new things. If you pile on days of eating unfamiliar foods, your body will rebel against you.

MOSQUITOES

SHARKS AND CHUCK NORRIS

ain't got shit on mosquitoes, the deadliest creature in the world and responsible for over one million deaths annually. In the States, these guys are just biters, but overseas they can be lethal or, at the very least, make your life miserable for days—if not longer. Mosquitoes carry malaria, dengue fever, encephalitis, and yellow fever, amongst other grizzly shit. If you're going to a tropical area with known mosquito issues, you'll need clothing that will cover you from head to toe and some serious repellant. If you're really hoofing it into the jungle, bring mosquito netting to sleep safely. And talk to the doctor about antimalarials—people from all over the world die every day from malaria transmitted by mosquitoes. They might be tiny, but they're serious.

TRAVEL INSURANCE

IF SHIT HITS THE FAN, HAVING

travel insurance is a good backup plan. It's basically protection for when the "what if" turns into reality. The issue with insurance is, we never know if or when those risks will materialize, and it's pretty likely you might buy insurance and never use it—which can feel like you've wasted some hard-earned dough. So what do you do?

Well, here's the deal: you know that traveling poses higher risks in all regards, health and safety being two risks that dominate the pool. Buying insurance can help ease your mind. For example, if you need to be immediately evacuated back home for treatment, you will be covered. Oftentimes, insurance will cover theft of almost anything and even the annoying accidents that happen along the way, like dropping your phone into the Seine while trying to get a photo. Think about your worst-case scenario and how much that would cost . . . and then decide if you want to get insurance. Check out WorldNomads.com and TravelGuard.com for some quotes and see what is covered. If you're worried about theft, accidents, or other trip interruptions, make sure those are included in your policy.

KEEPING YOUR JUNK SPOTLESS

WHEN YOU'RE LIVING THE backpacking dream, your daily itinerary can include things like cliff jumping, dive-bar crawling, and hostel fornicating. The last thing on your mind is genital hygiene. But there comes a time when your junk could really use some personal attention, and there's more to protecting your goods than not touching your wiener with curry-hands. While none of us are doctors, we all definitely have genitalia, and here is what we know about keeping your tools tidy while traveling.

Keep It Clean

The backpacking community is notorious for random hookups. With so many players in the game, it's important to make sure your equipment is clean and odor-free. Keep the home runs coming with regular showers. Just don't wash yourself raw—scrubbing too hard can cause infection. While your inner-hippie might be tempted to let your pubes grow wild, bear in mind that longer hair means more bacterial growth, which leads to funkier smells. In less-developed countries, getting a wax can be insanely cheap. Take advantage of it and go for that lightning bolt landing strip you've always wanted.

Ladies: the tighter your panties (or pants), the higher your risk of getting a yeast infection. Stick to cotton underwear, or if you're feeling ballsy, go commando. Bidets are a norm in lots of countries, so use these magic inventions to give your kitty an extra-good cleaning (or to make her purr if the water pressure's good). Stay away from douches though—like over-scrubbing, these can also cause infection.

OTP TIP: Baby wipes are super-handy for cleaning up more than babies.

Play It Safe

Backpackers are an adventurous bunch—especially in the sack—but don't get carried away and ride bareback. No matter how good your traveler's insurance is, the only coverage for avoiding an STD is to always wrap it up. It takes two to screw—girls should carry condoms, as well. Keep in mind that the risks are different across the world and that not all STDs are visible. Before getting on the plane at all, get tested. Not only is it good karma, but you can get properly treated for any infections at home instead of at some shady clinic in rural South America.

Where to Get the Goods

It's not a bad idea to pick up a big box of condoms at home—it'll be a hell of a lot lighter than the consequences of going without. If you opt to buy them abroad, pick a brand you've heard of and check the expiration date. You'll be able to find them in just about any drugstore, or if you're on a really tight budget, ask around for clinics or hostels that give them away for free. In some countries, it's frowned upon (or even illegal) for a lady to buy a condom, so look up condom laws before you go. In some cities in the Philippines, for example, no one can buy a condom without a prescription.

UTIs (Urinary Tract Infections)

Normally, these are much more common in women than men. On the road, people tend to get dehydrated from frequent movement and avoidance of contaminated water. Combine this with grimier conditions, and you got yourself a Grade A UTI. Point is: *drink lots of water*. If you can't find bottled water, use water treatment tablets, which kill most of the evil bastards that will give you the shits and nervous giggles. Pee as often as possible, even if it means popping a squat in a nearby bush. Holding it keeps bacteria trapped in your system and can lead to UTIs. If you're prone, get your doctor to prescribe a course of antibiotics before you go, just in case.

Birth Control

If you're a pill-popper, get your prescription filled before leaving and make sure it's enough for the whole trip. Keep an alarm set to the time back home so you know exactly when to take it upon arrival—it can get confusing with time-zone changes and long-ass flights. Taking the pill can be a pain when you're on the road, so consider switching to another form of birth control such as the NuvaRing, Depo-Provera, or the patch. Traveler's antibiotics (like the antimalarial doxycycline) can make the pill less effective, so bring rubber backup.

In Case of an Accident

Shit happens. Oral contraceptives can fail, and condoms can slip or break, turning a sloppy one-night stand in Barcelona into a *Knocked Up*-style fiasco. Luckily, the morning-after pill (emergency contraception/EC) is now available in over 140 countries. Check out what EC is available by country before you go, including what's sold over the counter. Remember that EC is only effective for 120 hours (five days) after an accident, and the longer you wait, the less powerful it is. If you're too late for the morning-after pill and can't handle a kid yet, look up the nearest family planning clinic and see what your options are for an abortion. Since abortion is illegal in many places, you may have to travel to another country or return home early.

SAFETY

EVERY COUNTRY HAS DIFFER- ent levels of general safety (i.e., likelihood of you getting robbed or hurt). While major crimes do happen, it's unlikely you'll be held up at gunpoint. As fun as a good pistol-whipping might sound, backpackers are normally seen as targets for petty theft and small-time crime. The things working against you:

- Your huge, necessary-but-obvious backpack.
- Petty criminals are well aware of the fact that backpackers will have more cash on them than most

locals. One stereotype about Americans (among many others) abroad is that they're rich.

- You will look (and will sometimes be) lost (especially if you're unfolding and looking at a giant map).
- You don't speak the language.
- You sleep in train stations (or on trains), on buses, or on beaches to save money—or because you're damn tired from recent travels.
- Being drunk or high. When you're impaired, the chance that you'll lose your belongings is greatly increased. Criminals know this.
- You see great things, and you take pictures of those things. People see your camera, and people want your camera.
- You're conspicuously messing around on your phone in public— which is like saying, "Here, take my phone. I'm obviously too stupid to have one."
- Hostels attract a wide variety of characters. Most are awesome, while others would love to relieve you of your possessions.

Here's the reality—as safe as you might feel, you have to be aware that you're always a target. This doesn't mean you should be a twitchy, paranoid mess, but be conscious of your surroundings and take precautions with your valuables.

Protect Your Shit
COPY/SCAN DOCUMENTS

People steal passports because they are worth a lot of money on the black market. So, make three copies of everything (legal ID, passport, birth certificate). Keep one copy on you, one in your backpack, and leave one with a trusted friend or family member. Scan all your documents and e-mail them to yourself. That way, even if you are robbed and stripped naked, you can still easily access and print out your documents. Another easy precautionary measure is to e-mail yourself necessary telephone numbers of your credit card companies (in case cards are stolen), hostels/airlines you've made reservations with, your bank, doctor, and family/friends.

PROTECT THE BACKPACK

With your backpack on your back, it's pretty easy for thieves to unzip, grab, and run. If you're napping somewhere where you might be vulnerable, use your pack as a pillow, and wrap the extra straps around your wrists. That way, if someone tugs, you'll feel it. If you're walking somewhere you feel particularly unsafe, wear your pack on your front to keep a closer eye on it. It will look like you're in your third trimester, but it's better than having to replace something important.

TRAVEL LOCKS

Buy a lock to secure your important items in hostels. Hostels usually provide you with lockers, but not locks. It's nice to know your stuff is safe when you're out getting cultured. Travel Sentry (Travelsentry.org) locks are made specifically with travelers in mind and offer designs for different scenarios. They fit on hostel lockers and your backpack zipper lock, as well. They are also recognized and easily opened by U.S. and U.K. customs officials at all airports. (If they're going to dig through your bag anyway, you might as well make it a faster process.)

INTUITION, ATTITUDE, AND COMMON SENSE

Stay alert and street-smart while traveling. You have to be assertive and avoid looking nervous, as schemers will exploit that instantly. Be aware of your surroundings and do not ask strangers to watch your stuff—take it with you even if it's for a quick bathroom break. Do some research on sketchy city regions to avoid, but don't get yourself to a point where you cut off your interaction with locals or deny yourself the ability to take your plans off course.

Avoid old baby mamas and their babies (or cute little begging kids for that matter). They often use their cuteness, helplessness, and desperation as a decoy to pick the pockets of tourists. Ignore them, check behind you, and walk away quickly.

M&M (MINIMIZE AND MONETIZE)

Minimize: Take as little as possible with you when you go out so you have less to carry and less that can be stolen. When going out, take what you need out of your wallet rather than bringing your whole wallet.

Monetize (i.e., keep your eyes on your money): Check often to make sure you don't have anything sticking out of your pockets (which is easier to do with less stuff). Try not to carry anything in your back pockets. Since your backside is mostly a layer of fat (it's true), you don't feel as much there, which makes reaching into your back pocket the easiest way for someone to snatch something.

NECK WALLETS AND MONEY BELTS

Neck wallets and money belts are options if you are extra paranoid about the safety of your documents (they're very nerd-chic; maybe more nerd than chic). These are slim pouches that you wear as a necklace or around your waist under your clothes, that can only fit your passport, some emergency cash, and a condom or two (although if you're wearing this, your chances of getting laid diminish significantly). While these things are decidedly unsexy, they can prevent passport theft, because even the most accomplished thieves find it difficult to reach up or down your shirt or pants without you noticing.

Political Unrest/ Civil War

Many countries are currently in a civil war, are politically unstable, and/or have regular violent protests. Being caught up in a politically fueled situation you are unfamiliar with can be dangerous. Tourists can be kidnapped, caught in crossfire, or just unable to escape the country. Read up on your destination's political climate and decide if visiting it at the moment would be a good idea. However, don't let previous civil unrest stop you from visiting a place, either. Countries like Burundi and Rwanda experienced civil unrest and genocide less than two decades ago but are now great places for an off-track adventure. Cross-reference The United States' Travel Portal and Australia's Travel Advisory to get a wider picture of travel advisories around the world.

The Police

Unfortunately a country's police force isn't always there to keep you safe—and sometimes, it's just the opposite. Corruption within government agencies is not uncommon abroad, and many government officials are openly willing to accept bribes. They also know you want to avoid trouble, so cops can be (and sometimes expect to be) paid off. For most developed countries, the police should be approachable, but it's a good idea, particularly when traveling in less developed areas, to ask the locals about the police force—and what alternatives you have if you do encounter an emergency.

Cab Drivers

Cab drivers are frequent scammers. Since a cab is often a luxury (or a necessity after a long day of travel), here are a few tips to keep you from getting scammed by cabbies:

- Insist on a meter or a set price before you get in the cab. In some countries, meters just aren't used, and if that's the case, negotiate the price before the taxi starts moving. It's also a good idea, if you know you'll be taking a cab to a well-known destination, to ask some locals what that route should cost.

- If you're nervous about hailing a random cab, call your hostel/hotel and ask them to call a reputable company and have them meet you at a designated location.

- While you're in the cab, be aware of the route you're taking. If you have a smartphone and a data plan, follow the cab on a map app like Google Maps. Otherwise, get a city map and follow along. This will help to ensure your cabbie isn't taking you for a ride to get more cash—and feel free to insist on a certain route in advance or while you're on your way.

- In countries where the risk of kidnapping is greater, following the route on a map will give you your bearings, and if you start to feel something is wrong, you can jump out and take off. Always make sure the door handles work from the inside, as well, and don't put your bag in the trunk; keep it with you in the backseat for a quick exit.

- Use dedicated taxi lines. In some places, unlicensed or unregulated taxi drivers will approach you and offer you a ride. Most cities have designated taxi lines where the properly licensed taxi drivers will line up.

- If a cabbie asks you if this is your first time in the city, your answer is always "no." Tell him or her that you've been here many times, and stop the conversation. While some drivers might just be chatty, others are trying to determine if they can circle the block a few times knowing you won't notice.

- Have small-currency bills or coins ready. Some cabbies will try and scam you with incorrect change for large bills.

Protect Your Technology

These days you have to protect your files and identity as well as your actual computer or phone. Passwords and bank account information travels over open networks, unfolding all of your digital personals for everyone to see and use. Check out CrashPlan +, proXPN, and TrueCrypt. These software companies are like a padlock for your digital information.

Your best bet is to leave your expensive gadgets at home. Buy a cheap, jailbroken cell phone that you wouldn't mind losing. Acer has inexpensive netbooks that are great for e-mail on the road and are super-lightweight and small, making them perfect for travel.

HOSTELS
and COUCHES

AS MUCH AS YOU MAY FIGHT IT, AT SOME POINT, YOU'RE going to need to get some sleep. As a backpacker, booking a hostel bed is your best chance to meet other young, single, like-minded travelers. Another rapidly growing option is CouchSurfing, a site on which you can connect with locals from a massive, worldwide, online community, who will allow you to stay at their home for no cost, often giving you great insider perspective of their city. Camping gives you the ultimate flexibility and can cost nothing. Bottom line: you're young, low-maintenance, and looking for fun—leave the five-star hotels for retirement and explore the broke-ass hostel accommodation options instead.

HOSTELS

HOSTELS ARE LOW-BUDGET accommodations normally set up like dormitories. In a hostel, you typically rent a bed, as opposed to in hotels, where you rent a room. Dorms usually have four to eight beds, but single or double private rooms could be available, and dorms can sometimes be much bigger. (The hostel on Beachcomber Island in Fiji has a 120-bed dorm!) They range from modern, resort-like, hedonistic party palaces with gorgeous views, sexy young backpackers, and a fully stocked cheap bar to undecorated dens set up solely for sleeping purposes. At the very least, a bed, pillow, community bathroom, and basic security will be provided.

Hostel Pros
CROWD

An international collection of young, sexy, and broke backpackers makes the hostel scene worth your traveling dollars. Since the turnover at hostels is so high, everyone is always welcoming to newcomers. Intense friendships (and then some) form quickly since you skip a few steps between being strangers and coinhabitants.

PRICE

Typically, beds run $15 to $30 per night, but can be as cheap as $2 to $3 in Asia or Central America. Many hostels have on-site bars with the cheapest drinks in town. Sure, you may not get a mint on your pillow, but you'll be sitting next to a smiling

hot young Aussie drinking a $2 caipirinha instead of an old suit staring at his phone and sipping a $14 cognac at a hotel bar.

STAFF

Hostel employees are usually backpackers, young locals, or both. They have the best insider info for cheap food, sites, and bars, and will often join you. If you need to go to the airport, a hostel worker will bust out a map, outline which metro lines to take, and tell you exactly how much it will cost. By comparison, a hotel concierge will call you a taxi and stand patiently (or impatiently) until you tip him.

Hostel Cons
PRIVACY

You don't get much "me" space in a hostel. Bathrooms are usually the only private areas, but it's all you need. You're here to be social, and bumping into a girl when she's changing her pants is a great icebreaker.

PRICE

Yes, it's much cheaper than hotels, but in midsummer, European dorm beds can cost an extortionate $75. Free is cheaper—see CouchSurfing (next page).

LACK OF LOCAL CULTURE

If you get tied up in a party hostel with a great crowd, it's easy to forget to explore the city you're in. Don't let a week of debauchery with other gringos at a hostel in Buenos Aires ever keep you from saying "*una empanada, por favor*" or hitting on at least one porteño (local lass).

BEDBUGS

Every backpacker's worst nightmare—and not just because they attack in your sleep—these bloodsuckers live in mattresses and couches and are the size of seeds you'd pick out of a bag of schwag. Check recent hostel reviews to make sure there's no infestation. But if you do wake with what look like mosquito bites in odd places (usually in groups of three), tell the hostel manager, wash all your clothes in hot water, and get the fuck out of there. The problem isn't unique to hostels, but the constant travel and communal environments help spread the critters.

Booking

If you are traveling in high season, have a tight schedule, and want to stay at the highest-rated hostels, you may need to book four to six weeks in advance. Otherwise, a couple of days prior should be sufficient, and sometimes, you can just walk in and find a bed. Hostels may have last-minute openings, beds they don't list online, or couches or hammocks you can crash on for a few bucks. There are plenty of booking and hostel review websites to help you find a crash pad.

Helpful Hostel Tips

BARGAIN, FOO

If you are traveling in a large group or plan to stay for more than a couple nights, ask for a discounted rate. It never hurts, and it works surprisingly often.

GET CARDED

If you're on a longer trip, a Hosteling International or other hostel alliance membership card will pay itself off quickly.

PLUG UP

If you're a light sleeper, bring earplugs and an eye mask. People are generally respectful of sleepers in the dorms, but occasionally someone has an early flight, gets a little too drunk and stumbles around the room, fidgets with an unruly plastic bag, or makes the bunks squeak after finding love for the night.

SAFETY

We've stayed in hundreds of hostels and have yet to be hacked to bits. You'll be fine; just take care of your shit. Hostels provide lockers for your bags or at least your valuables (so bring a lock!), or they'll hold them in a safe at reception. Backpackers are generally very respectful of each others' things, so it's rarely a problem, but play it safe.

COUCHSURFING

THE CONCEPT SEEMS TOO shady to be true: you send a message to a local in the city you plan to visit, and he/she invites you to be a guest in his/her home. Well, it's real. With over five million members worldwide, CouchSurfing is a free-to-use network that connects travelers with locals and allows travel enthusiasts to safely flop around on each others' international couches. Sign up as a host, a surfer, or both. If you play the game well, you can get a free place to sleep with the added benefit of a local's perspective on your destination—something you can't always find in a hostel. A general "pay it forward" undertone exists with the hope that you'll host CouchSurfers in your city when you eventually move out of your parents' basement.

CouchSurfing Pros
IT'S FREE

Not "free, but gratuity accepted" free, or "free, but you can repay me tonight . . . wink, wink" free, but actually free. Monetary payment is strictly prohibited in the CouchSurfing community, but it's common to find creative ways to give something back.

HOSTS

The generous CouchSurfing hosts are normally locals or at least residents who know the area. Usually, they'll have great insider recommendations and may invite you to hang out with some of their local friends. Be grateful. These wallet saviors make CouchSurfing possible.

COMMUNITY

CouchSurfers in most cities coordinate budget gatherings or events for local and traveling CSers, and many hosts accommodate several surfers at once. Also, CouchSurfers are often the brokest of the broke travelers. So if your dinner budget calls for eating crackers in the park, you may find company. The profile count is several million strong and growing. Couch-Surfers exist in every country on the planet, and they're normally down to at least meet up and talk shop.

CouchSurfing Cons
NOT THE BACKPACKER PARTY CROWD

CouchSurfers are a solid, entertaining group that occasionally party with the best of 'em, but the day-in and day-out hookups and guaranteed debauchery of a party hostel isn't part of the community (which can be a "pro" when your liver needs a rest). Sometimes you may be on your own with a busy, working host, so you'll have to entertain yourself. And, unlike hostel backpackers, CSers come in all ages and walks of life.

RANGE OF COMFORT

You may get lucky finding someone with a spare bedroom, but usually you're sleeping on a floor mat or (surprise!) a couch in the living room. The host's profile will list the sleeping arrangements, so you'll know what to expect.

Booking

This takes some prep time. You'll first need to set up a profile, post pictures and information about yourself, and get references from past travel buddies. When your profile is ready, search for hosts in your destination preferably a week in advance (more in high season). Review the profiles to make sure the location, couch, and host are all to your liking. Download the CouchSurfing app to stay on top of the dialogue.

Safety

You are in someone's home, so your stuff should be as safe as everything they own. As for the dilemma of sleeping at a stranger's home, the self-policing of CouchSurfing's active community keeps it very safe—just remember to use common sense. If some dude has a new profile, no friends or recommendations, a picture that resembles Hannibal Lecter, and asks that all CouchSurfing requests include a picture of your feet, you might want to pass. But if your potential host has plenty of recommendations (especially from others in your demographic), an interesting profile, and has been an active member of the community for a while, you should have nothing to worry about.

MORE OPTIONS

Apartment Rental

When the hostels in a city are booked and there are no couches left to surf, renting an apartment is often still an option. The fast-growing site Airbnb.com makes it easy. You can rent entire apartments or share with a host (like a paid version of Couch-Surfing). This is also useful for bigger groups or if you're planning on bringing back local tail and the hostels have a "guests only" policy.

Camping

For the ultimate freedom while back-packing, pitch a tent. Camping connects you to international wilderness and can save you big bucks. Just check the local ordinances and stay away from the bums and tweekers. In Scandinavia, there is actually a "right to access" law that allows you to camp on any land, public or private, as long as it's not being farmed and you don't get in people's way. If you buy your gear locally, you'll save your back from lugging it across the world and possibly on baggage fees. The equipment isn't cheap, but it will quickly pay for itself in saved accommodations costs. You can also sell it online once you're all camped-out.

Hotels

While hotels generally aren't the ideal option, occasionally they make sense. On some islands in Thailand, it costs $2 for a hostel bed or $10 for a private room in a resort with a pool.

After months of travel, it's nice to treat yourself and sprawl out naked on a double bed for a few nights (especially if you've found a travel fling). Just remember to return to the backpacker grime before your hands get too soft.

SEX, DRUGS, and PARTYING

THERE ARE LOTS OF FUN WAYS TO FIND YOURSELF ABROAD, but this part is the most fun to discuss. Sex, drugs, and partying will make your trip memorably mind-blowing and are vital to your worldly experience. You will be hooking up with a whole slew of internationals, and you will have a damn good time doing it (safely, of course). If some drugs find their way on the menu, we won't judge. Moderation is always key (nobody likes a crackhead). As for partying, there are beach parties, club parties, hostel, hot-tub, and pool parties for the taking abroad. Here are a few things we have learned along the way that should maximize your fun times.

SEX

THE CONDITIONS ABROAD are perfect for getting laid. Everyone is so excited to be out of their element that any inhibitions are left far behind. Hooking up with fellow backpackers is inevitable. They're just as horny and are in the same boat with you mentally (sometimes even close to the same bed). Hooking up with locals is more of a challenge, but everybody loves a good chase, right? A few important factors to get you laid by a local:

• **Looking your best** abroad may be hard. Groom, shower, and primp a bit if you plan to get laid. Go grungy when you're in between places. Balance is key.

• **Smile and be friendly.** Sure, the mysterious character is cool, if you think you can play it—just save that card as the ace up your sleeve.

• **Conversate.** Talk about where you're from and how much you love traveling. Good conversation skills, even in a language you're not familiar with, are charming.

• **Modify your tactics** based on your location. Buying drinks and generally being awesome always helps, but knowing a bit of the local ways and hot spots won't hurt your cause.

• **Culture matters** when it comes to sex. Some places are very lenient on the sexual liberation front. Other places, like the Middle East, have very strict hook-up rules, and premarital sex may be out of the question altogether.

To get more in the know, here's a list of some our favorite spots for sneaking in a quickie:

Berlin, Germany

The newest ingredients make this cultural melting pot worth a taste. Warehouse clubs, grungy districts, and hidden bars give Berlin's large S&M crowds proper grounds to play.

Santorini, Greece

Nude beaches, hot backpackers, and world-famous sunsets will help bring some romance back into your stick-it-where-it-fits sex life.

Kuala Lumpur, Malaysia

Malaysians bring kink back into the bedroom and the beach. Just don't frown if there's a price—what comes next will be well worth the coin.

Ibiza, Spain

The mecca of electronic music, Ibiza is where you can get your dance on all night, then settle into your beach-side shack for some good lovin' before sunrise.

Stockholm, Sweden

The Nordic are naughty. With its beautiful, busty blonde babes and tall, large-handed dudes, the Swedes have been ranked as the most bisexual in the world. We're always down for trying new things.

Warsaw, Poland

This capital city hosts an annual Eroticon Festival. Enough said.

São Paulo, Brazil

Big booties shake with pride in the thong's birthplace. Unleash your desires on the beach or bring it back to one of the city's hundreds of luxurious sex motels with rental rates by the hour.

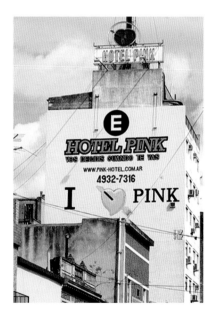

Global Street Smart Chart

	LEGAL DRINKING AGE	AGE OF CONSENT	MARIJUANA LAW	PROSTITUTION LAWS
UNITED STATES	**NONE – 21** Legal age to purchase is 21 in all states	**16–18**	**PARTIALLY LEGAL** Decriminalization and medical usage is legal in 23 states	**ILLEGAL** IN ALL BUT ONE STATE... Nevada (Viva Las Vegas baby!)
THAILAND	**18**	**18**	**EXTREMELY ILLEGAL** Death penalty is possible for drug offenses	**ILLEGAL, BUT...** Tolerated & partly regulated
NETHERLANDS	**16/18** 16 = wine & beer with less than 15% alcohol content 18 = all liquor	**16**	**LEGAL, BUT...** Tourists are no longer allowed to legally make purchases	**LEGAL** and regulated
AUSTRALIA	**18**	**16–18**	**PARTIALLY LEGAL** Decriminalized in some states	**LEGAL** With restrictions in certain territories
COLOMBIA	**18**	**14**	**PARTIALLY LEGAL** Decriminalized for possession of small amounts	**LEGAL** In designated "tolerance zones"
INDIA	**18–25** Varies between states. Consumption in some states is prohibited	**14/16** Male / Female	**PARTIALLY LEGAL** Used during observance of certain Hindu rituals	**LEGAL** But soliciting in a public place and pimping are outlawed
RUSSIA	**NONE** No legal drinking age, but selling alcohol to minors is prohibited	**16**	**PARTIALLY LEGAL** Possession of up to 6 grams is punishable by fines	**ILLEGAL, BUT...** Not considered a serious crime
AFGHANISTAN	**ILLEGAL** Those who buy, sell, or consume alcohol can be fined or imprisoned	**18/MARRIED** Male / Female	**ILLEGAL** Though heavily trafficked on the black market	**ILLEGAL** Punishments range from 5 to 15 years of imprisonment
NORTH KOREA *uncited claim	**18**	***15** *Statements claim sex is not permitted outside marriage	***ILLEGAL** Statements claim marijuana is heavily grown and trafficked to help support the country's economy	**ILLEGAL** According to the North Korean government, prostitution does not exist, but is practiced discreetly

DRUGS

TRAVELING IS GOING TO

get you feeling all kinds of good. Amidst the partying, exploring, and meeting of all kinds of people, there may come a time when you want to take your experience to an even higher level. We won't pack your bowl, draw your line, or strap your arm (hopefully it doesn't come to that), but we are here to help.

Substance Specifics

Amsterdam was once a liberal land that welcomed and catered to pot-smoking tourists with coffee shops that were legally slangin' dubs left and right. Things are changing a bit, but the people's habits remain. Marijuana is a celebrated soft drug that varies in regard around the world. The United States is loosening its shackles on possessing small amounts, but you still wouldn't want to get caught with a couple grams of sticky. Some countries have completely decriminalized pot, while others will lock you up in a heartbeat. As with everything, be careful and know the local laws.

OPTION A

Your best bet: ask people you know. Hostel mates, especially, but anybody you've come into friendly contact with will suffice. Just work the question into a smooth conversation to see if they can help you out.

OPTION B

A bit more risky: ask unfamiliar people. As with your first choice, try to make friendly conversation first. This lowers your chance of getting straight-up robbed, and (with enough conversational knowledge) should help you weed out the out-of-uniform cops. Drugs tend to follow the money. Stick around nightlife—bars and clubs especially—and ask patrons, bartenders, or bouncers. You could start off by asking for pot (as its use is generally taken more lightly). If that goes well, feel free to shmooze your way into inquiring about some other stuff.

All kinds of drugs will be available everywhere, and their legality will vary from place to place. Take precaution in buying or using.

PARTYING

A PARTY IS TO BE HAD ANY- where in the world. Your entire experience abroad is going to blend into one big party, and you can find something that fits your specific moods and needs in every country. Some will be organized annual celebrations, others impromptu park and house parties or in the ever-present clubs, bars—even costume balls (during the day, night, morning, and any time in between). A taste of some big guns awaiting your arrival:

- Oktoberfest in Germany (page 103) (around September 20 to October 10, annually) is an organized shitshow dedicated to international beer consumption and downright messiness.

- Carnaval in Brazil (page 105) (February 22 to 28, annually) is known worldwide for flooding the Rio's streets with its elaborate costumes (with built-in nakedness) and wild celebrations.

- Botellóns in Spain (page 112) are organized park drinking parties. You bring your booze, everyone else brings their booze, and you share. Most large plazas in Spain will hold one around 10 p.m. every weekend night.

- Australia Day (January 26th) is where the country (well, continent) celebrates the discovery (through European settlement) of Australia. It's all about beers, barbecues, and beaches.

- Full Moon Parties in Thailand (page 114) (every full moon) celebrate the lunar phase by bringing a bangin' party to Ko Pha Ngan's beaches. DJs and drinks will keep you dancing until the sun comes up.

- Holi (typically the third week in March) is a multiday Hindu tradition that takes food fighting to a grown-up level. Massive crowds flood the streets while dousing each other with colorful flour. India serves it up strongest.

Part Three

MAKE YOURSELF USEFUL

BACKPACKING IS A LEARNING EXPERIENCE ALL ON ITS OWN. You'll interact with a multitude of cultures on an intimate level, digging deep to see how people really live. When you decide it's time to add even more value to your vagabonding (or if you just want to give yourself a reason to stay longer), consider working, studying, or volunteering abroad. The best approach to applying yourself while traveling is to first pin down what you're most interested in. Have a soft spot for kids? You can educate the next generation of adults by volunteering to teach English, sports, or crafty skills in almost any place around the world. If you're all about keeping our planet green, cuddling endangered species, helping to alleviate the impact of disease and fighting for human rights, we've got something for you to get passionately involved in. We're recommending some of our favorite programs, schools, and employers— sorted by areas of interest—to give you a taste of the endless opportunities available worldwide.

ANIMALS

ANIMALS AROUND THE WORLD SUFFER, MAINLY BECAUSE of humans, and there are many ways to use your petting hand for something more meaningful. If you can grow a beard, you can save bears in Asia, supersize your love for felines in South America, and do it like Darwin in the Galapagos. Pick your favorite four-legger (two or none-legger also work), pack a squeaky toy, and get yourself in a furry situation.

BUSKING FOR BEARS

YOU CAN BE ALL ABOUT THE yin and yang, but some weird shit goes into traditional Asian medicines. Dog meat is a common street treat, and drinking tiger penis brew is nothing new. Needless to say, it's tough to be fuzzy in Asia. Moon bears have it especially rough. A critically endangered species, these teddies are housed in small cages and farm-raised, then slaughtered for their stomach bile, which is thought to have some medicinal superpowers. Jill Robinson, a pissed-off animal lover, started the Animals Asia Foundation (AAF) in 1998 to help these bears (and other mistreated animals) by organizing interesting, fund-, and awareness-raising projects.

Busking and Yoga and Beards, Oh Shit!

While their missions may be similar, AAF kicks PETA's ass in the sense-of-humor department. In 2010, AAF rallied Hong Kong's best buskers—a rag-tag bunch of the city's jammiest street musicians—for an event called Buskers for Bears. In 2011, bear enthusiasts stretched it out at Yoga for Bears, and 2012 got a little hairy with the Beards for Bears campaign. The goal of all this madness was to raise money to get bears out of cages and into an AAF rehabilitation center.

The Outcome

Apparently, buskers and beards actually work for bears! Since 1998, AAF has signed agreements regarding the protection of moon bears with both the Chinese and Vietnamese governments; rescued 700 bears from an organ-farmed future; and aided in the closing of more than forty Chinese bear farms. As a way to keep everyone happy, the AAF gives the medicine man his due by providing cruelty-free alternatives for bile in traditional brews.

Save a Bear with Your Facial Hair

AAF has three major programs—End Bear Farming, Cat and Dog Welfare (to end cat and dog eating), and Action Against Cruelty. World headquarters are in Hong Kong, and there are Moon Bear Rescue Centers in Vietnam and China. AAF is always looking for self-motivated volunteers to organize fundraising events and street collections. While some animal-focused volunteer programs are more like a petting zoo, AAF continues to innovate their approaches to raising awareness for their causes. And you thought your beard was only good for storing bits of lunch until dinner.

BEST PLACES TO BIRDWATCH FOR CREDITS

THE WORLD HAS MUCH TO offer if you're a bird nerd or just into checking out wildlife beyond the squirrels at your local park. Studying ecology abroad exposes you to indigenous species you may not find at home and places you in the cultural thick of it, allowing you to scope out ecosystems while you get to know the people who inhabit them, all while racking up credits.

Ecuador's Blue Boobies

Ecuador is home to the blue-footed booby, a bird with super-blue feet (but no Pamela Ds, unfortunately). Thanks to a partnership between Boston University and Universidad San Francisco de Quito in Ecuador, you can get credits toward your ecology degree while studying some of the world's most coveted endemic species. This intensive, semester-long program offers students a chance to get their hands filthy in three completely different ecosystems—montane forest, tropical rainforest, and coastal habitats—while simultaneously learning Spanish. Not only do you get to study for four weeks in the Amazon, but they also hook you up with an eight-day trip to the Galapagos Islands, the animal inhabitants of which inspired a little theory you may have heard about. There, you can do like Darwin and witness the mating rituals of the waved albatross and make friends with all kinds of tortoises and iguanas.

Batshit Crabby

The archipelago hangs out in the Indian Ocean on the Eastern coast of North Africa and is made up of Pemba Island and Zanzibar, along with a bunch of tiny little islets. While the islands are not as biodiverse as mainland Africa, the shrews, monkeys, mongooses, and colorful lizards here will still blow your mind. To give your animal escapades some structure, sign up for the SIT Study Abroad Program (Sit.edu). During the fifteen-week course, you get to shoot the shit in Swahili during one of two homestays on Pemba—where you can observe the rare, endemic Pemba fruit bats in action. Plan on setting aside some quality time with the red colobus monkeys during an excursion to the Jozani Forest, and then go snorkel crazy on the underwater wildlife off the islets of Bawe, Changuu, Misali, Mbudya, and Sinda. Once you resurface, don't think you're trippin' balls when the boulders grow claws. The coconut crab is the largest arthropod in the world and crawls around these shores making other crabs look like bird food (and it also eats meat sometimes).

Visit These Animals Before They're Fossils

MAGELLANIC PENGUIN

Named after Magellan, these are the largest penguins in the world. Instead of the tuxedo getup, they sport a horseshoe pattern and shed their eye feathers during the warm months.

Endangered because ... their fishy food supply is currently being threatened by overfishing, and they waddle into fishing nets and get covered in oil.

Still kickin' it in ... Argentina, Chile, Falkland Islands

COLOMBIAN WOOLLY MONKEY

Fuzzy and woolen, these monkeys use their incredibly strong tails to swing through the Amazon with ease. What have you done with your third limb lately?

Endangered because ... fewer trees in the Amazon means fewer branches on which to swing in avoidance of predators—like jaguars, eagles, and humans—who snatch them up and sell them illegally as pets.

Still kickin' it in ... Colombia, Venezuela

SCHMIDT'S LAZY TOAD

The true embodiment of the toad, these frogs are terribly ugly, with warts dotting their bodies, long, lanky legs, and see-through underbellies. They mostly live on land, shamefully hiding under rocks until mating season, where they pop into the water for a quickie.

Endangered because ... they're actually pretty lazy (or rather, confined to a small area where they thrive). Since their habitat is so limited, and their numbers small, any change to their environment may wipe them out for good.

Still kickin' it in ... Southern and Central China

BLUE BUSTARD

Like an obese tenor, this bird has the voice of a frog and makes little croaking sounds to communicate with other bustards in the bunch.

Endangered because ... the more we mow down their home turf, the less they can croak around freely.

Still kickin' it in ... South Africa, Lesotho

STRIPED LEG-LESS LIZARD

If a lizard has no legs, isn't it basically a snake? Science tells us that their evolutionary histories—snakes never had legs and legless lizards once did—distinguish them greatly.

Endangered because ... their habitat is being invaded by two-leggers with tractors, and these lizards don't like to slither on concrete.

Still kickin' it in ... Australia

BIG CATS OF THE AMAZON

THE SOUTH AMERICAN JUN-gles conjure up images of jaguars lurking in trees and cougars feasting on deer carcasses. But if you take a trip to the Amazon jungle or Pantanal, you'll have a tough time spotting them. They're not just being big pussies—these animals have been hunted to near extinction in the past century. Conservation efforts have stabilized their numbers, but deforestation, overhunting of their natural prey, and killing by local farmers to protect livestock keep their future uncertain. Black market dealings also still happen—big cats are hunted for their fur, and moms are killed and babies kidnapped to sell as exotic pets. Here's how to properly get your paws dirty to help these felines.

Comunidad Inti Wara Yassi (CIWY), Bolivia

In the 1980s, a couple of Bolivian kids saw firsthand the devastation from unregulated deforestation. At the same time, they witnessed widespread animal abuse—from malnourished circus cats to monkeys forced to get drunk and dance for locals. What started as a pinky swear between friends to protect animals and the environment has turned into an internationally acclaimed environmental conservation effort and an animal rescue and rehabilitation center. Today, CIWY has three sanctuaries where volunteers can work directly with big cats—feeding, walking, and caring for them. This is the best cougar action you'll find outside of a La Paz *boliche*.

Panthera, Brazil

The biggest and best big cat conservation effort in the world, Panthera is at the top of their kitty-saving game. Recently, when the government of Mongolia wanted to allow the hunting of some almost-extinct snow leopards for "research," Panthera fought back Genghis-hard and got the proposal overturned. Their South American branch is based in Brazil's Pantanal region, home to the largest concentration of jaguars in the world. Local farmers often shoot jaguars to protect their cattle herds, so Panthera is educating locals, observing jaguar behavior, and developing protected corridors and regions for the cats. They work on a wide scale with wild jaguars, so volunteer and work opportunities are more data collection, grant-writing, and necessary administrative duties than petting and taking pictures with jaguar kittens.

Beware!

Volunteers love the big cats, and every animal shelter knows this. Some opportunists actually keep cats around solely to attract volunteers, and volunteer dollars, rather than rehabilitating and rereleasing them. Don't get conned. Check various reviews online (not just the organization's website), or find a listing of trustworthy programs—VolunteerSouthAmerica.net is a great place to start.

DISEASE

WHILE WORKING TO HELP ALLEVIATE AIDS IS A WELL-publicized (and important) issue you can jump on abroad, hunger, lack of clean water, and various other diseases also affect the health of the world's population on a large scale. Opportunities are available in a wide array of settings, from hospitals to school clinics, healthcare offices to out in the field, and digging wells to create clean water supplies. While you don't need to be a doctor to help, if you're studying medicine, getting your bearings by working or volunteering abroad would add a lot of value to your MD résumé.

HALF FULL: CLEAN WATER VOLUNTEER PROGRAMS

OUR WORLD IS ROYALLY

screwed when it comes to water. One out of every eight people in the world don't have access to sufficient drinking water—that's nearly a billion. Some women and girls in Africa walk four hours each day to retrieve water, a hike that leaves them wide open for heat strokes and attacks by humans or animals. The time it takes to *just get water* makes it difficult to find time for schooling. What they do end up retrieving often resembles porta-potty slush—sometimes because it is. One out of every four people (two-fucking-billion!) in the world don't have a toilet. More people have cell phones than have toilets. This lethal combination of water shortage and contamination kills 9,000 people every day, one person every nine

seconds, or three million people a year. Half are children. These numbers are no doubt hard to swallow.

While the task of fixing this seems overwhelming, there are many organizations fighting the global water crisis. Wells are dug, boreholes are constructed, pumps are installed, pipes are laid, and new water-purification methods are constantly being tested and implemented. When looking to volunteer with an NGO (non-governmental organization), be sure they have funding transparency and ask about their sustainability plans. A water pump that breaks after nine months does a community no good if they have no mechanic, parts, or money to fix it. Here are a couple nonprofits to get your search started.

World Water Corps

World Water Corps (WWC)—the field division of Water for People (WaterForPeople.org)—researches communities and locations in developing nations that have a safe-water crisis. Data is collected and analyzed intensely to ensure a sustainable location is set up within a dedicated community. WWC not only makes it a point to engage the communities, but also relies *on them* 100 percent to dig the wells themselves and construct the latrines. It becomes a personal investment for everyone in the community, and not just a handout. WWC is on-site to monitor the entire operation, but in reality it becomes a project by the community, for the community. They have projects in developing nations worldwide and take volunteers for data collection, monitoring, and analysis of fieldwork. If you're more hands than numbers, volunteer for their Scoop program, where photojournalists shoot footage on-site and write and compose promotional materials for the Water for People marketing team.

Water.org

You may have seen commercials or online videos from this nonprofit, which features celebrities (Matt Damon is a cofounder) narrating videos that tug at your heart and ask for donations. Their focus is to raise awareness and funds for areas of the world that do not have safe drinking water or sanitation. They organize fundraisers and solicit donations, emphasizing that every small amount can help—just $25 can give someone water for life. Then they partner with local NGOs to organize and fund a sustainable water solution project that involves the community. The organization appeals to wallets, and we all know yours is empty. Instead, check their website for info about which current and future local NGOs they are sponsoring. Hit up those NGOs and find out how you can get on the ground and get your hands wet.

Water Missions International

Water Missions International +

Changing lives through sustainable water systems

This top-rated nonprofit has implemented safe water solutions in over forty-nine countries for more than two million people. While it is a Christian Engineering Ministry, you won't be doing any Bible thumping. Fieldwork is completely dedicated to engineering and implementing sustainable safe water projects, and they already have an impressive track record of doing so. WMI (WaterMissions.org) is well-funded because god-gobblers *love* giving to charities, and they are on track to being a global safe water-solutions leader. They conduct internships abroad and at the headquarters in Charleston, South Carolina.

BEST MD YOU CAN BE

GET YOUR PREMED

requisites out of the way while prodding the world and having a damn good time doing it. All the cultural knowledge you'll gather through foreign bar-hopping, city-touring, and sightseeing will do wonders for your bedside manner later in life. Before you commit most of your twenties to hitting the med-school books, check out our list of the best places to be while you're chasing your MD.

London

Pound for pound, London is becoming the strongest sale for studying abroad. Its history, style, entertainment, and entire experience will have your mind radiating with culture shock while the luxury of the same spoken language will keep you feeling comfortable enough to ask the waiter exactly what's in that scary-looking plate of pig's cheeks. Specific premed programs are set up in King's College—with focuses on biomedical sciences and clinical experience—and University College London, which hones in on international health policy studies.

Copenhagen

The Danish lifestyle is sweet as ever, and studying here is the best way to take a bite out of what the country's got to offer. The Danish Institute for Study Abroad (Disabroad.org) makes your transition to living and studying in Denmark easy, and Copenhagen's easy-going and friendly way of life

makes it fun. Plenty of medicine and health-policy programs offered by Denmark International Studies will keep you on your premed path, while the city's utopian transit system and easy inter-country connectivity will keep your more travel-minded path in check. You can even practice alternative medicines in Christiania, a small autonomous region of Copenhagen with chill policies on soft drugs.

Australia

Shake up your collegiate career by taking your studies Down Under. Not just cool for cuddly koalas and kangaroos, Australia's got plenty of sights to see and places to backpack while fulfilling the educational requirements to keep Mom and Dad (or whoever's floating the bill) satisfied. With one of the largest research institutions in the country, you can study grand-scale subjects like health and society or cultural studies in health at the University of Melbourne. Head to the nation's capital to study medicine with a close-to-home approach and sign up for classes at the University of Sydney, which offers courses in community and indigenous health.

India

The birthplace of *ayurveda* and the source of everything that's weird and interesting about alternative medicine, India is a great place for a med-head. Various programs are available in beachy Kerala, where you can watch locals prepare medicinal plants and smell the healing scents of ancient alternative medicine. For a more Western approach, check out the medical healthcare internships offered by Gap 360 (Gap360.com), a well-established company offering programs in various areas of study. Located in Palampur (the Dalai Lama's 'hood), this program is custom-tailored to medical and dental students seeking a unique understanding of the Indian healthcare system. Aside from the school-learnin', the program includes trips to the region's famed tea gardens, market tours, and weekly yoga and meditation to prep your nerves for medical school.

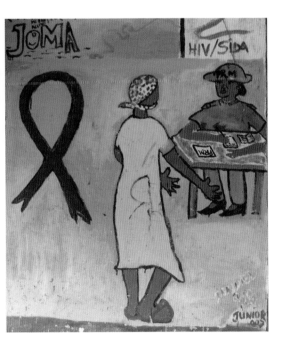

WHAT YOU CAN DO FOR AIDS RELIEF RIGHT NOW!

HIV/AIDS IS NO ONE-NIGHT stand. Most prevalent in Africa and Asia, this disease has affected every population around the world and continues to claim the lives of millions of people annually. While we're no longer in the midst of the '90s wave of awareness campaigns, there is still much work to be done to help those affected.

Advance-Africa

Available in either Tanzania or Kenya, these programs run from two weeks to six months. You can choose to work as a teacher at an orphanage or with an HIV/AIDS medical program. Med students and aspiring doctors are in top demand for the medical programs, and volunteers have the opportunity to do either lab research or hands-on medical work. In Kenya, Advance-Africa (Advance-Africa.com) offers travel programs that allow volunteers to assist in the remote villages of the Maasai tribe.

Worldwide Helpers

This U.K.-based company (WorldwideHelpers.org) has connected 17,000 do-gooders with low-cost or no-cost volunteerships around the world. Creating a free account with the organization gives you access to hundreds of great projects. Among them are a variety of HIV/AIDS education and community outreach programs in Africa.

AIDS Relief International (ARI)

Started by a group of kids who graduated from Brown University in 2011, ARI (AidsReliefInternational.org) focuses on the HIV-positive children of Mumbai. You know how a lot of medicine needs to be taken with food to be effective? Well, AIDS medication isn't any different. While some families in this region do have access to medicine, this charity aims to make sure they have the proper nutrition to make that medicine effective. Contact the organization for volunteer or employment opportunities both stateside and in India.

AIDS Relief for China (ARFC)

If you've got your own ideas about how to combat AIDS, ARFC (Arfcusa.org) is a charity that hooks up people on a mission with the funds necessary to make it possible. In 2004, ARFC worked with the Pen

Pal Kids Club to connect rural kids affected by HIV/AIDS with urban volunteers. In 2008, ARFC began facilitating Heart Talk support groups for gay men in more than thirty Chinese cities. You can either contact ARFC about volunteer opportunities with existing programs, or pitch your own charitable idea and apply for an ARFC grant to make it a reality.

Global Volunteer Network (GVN)

This organization was started in 2000 by a New Zealander who felt volunteer opportunities were far too limited by program fees. While GVN (GlobalVolunterNetwork.org) isn't directly focused on AIDS relief, they do offer many programs in the field and aim to place volunteers directly into communities in need of their specific skills. The Remote Orphan Care Project in rural Uganda is good for camp-counselor types, where volunteers help to organize games, assist with basic schooling, and provide age-appropriate AIDS education. The HIV/AIDS program in Kenya is a crash course in psychology, where volunteers help with homecare visits and counsel community groups. With all kinds of projects in fifteen countries, GVN's network includes some of the most interesting and hands-on volunteerships in the world.

KIDS

AS THE CLICHÉ GOES, "CHILDREN ARE OUR FUTURE." BY jumping into kid-centered work, study, and volunteer programs, you get to participate in the formative years of our world's population. Helping a child learn English, or just a few new soccer moves, may be the spark they need to lead a happy, productive life. Also, hanging out with kids is the best way to get insider intel on any given culture. Win, win.

BITTER CHOCOLATE: CHILD LABOR IN THE IVORY COAST

THERE'S A BITTER PROBLEM lingering around the production of chocolate. Cocoa farms in the Ivory Coast—which supply major companies like Hershey and produce over a third of the world's cocoa—enslave tens of thousands of kids as young as ten years old to crop their fields. Kids are overworked and beaten regularly, all in the name of turning cocoa beans into green. While the issue has gained some global awareness and caused consumer outrage, the major problem has not yet melted away.

What's Going On

At the turn of the millennium, the dark side behind chocolate was revealed, and the Cocoa Protocol came into effect, a program which aimed to eliminate child labor in cocoa production. Years later and leading up to today, children in the Ivory Coast and all along West Africa are still being forced to work 100-hour weeks at low (if any) pay cropping cocoa plantations. Some are ripped from or sold by their families while others voluntarily go, lured by the false promises of food and pay; many even arrive through the sex trade that spans the continent. Upon arrival at their "jobs," all of these children face regular beatings, starvation, and exhaustion while working in the fields.

Do Something

Mega companies like Hershey and Mars claim that tracing the sources of all of their products is next to impossible, which is why the problem persists. We think that's a shitty excuse, and here's how you can help:

STOP FUELING THE FIRE

Americans alone spend over $13 billion a year on chocolate, much of which comes from the Ivory Coast. Seek out Fair Trade chocolates instead, which are produced without slave labor—or just lay off the sweets. Some great-tasting, good-feeling companies include Equal Exchange, Madécasse, and Dagoba. The money is the motivator; until your dollar is missed, these mega companies won't soon change their methods.

GET OVER THERE

Put up against the standard of living in complete poverty, working in this environment seems like a more productive way of life. Uneducated, hungry, and poor, these children often opt for manual labor because no better option is available. Volunteer organizations are set up throughout the continent and are the best means through which you can give these kids something better to live for. Kids Worldwide (KidsWorldwide.org) is a unique organization that is approaching kid-focused development in Africa by cutting out the moneymaking middlemen who normally stand between you and volunteer projects. An organization run by volunteers for volunteers, Kids Worldwide "scaffolds" existing grassroots projects and helps develop them until they become self-sustainable, or for about five years.

As such, opportunities at Kids Worldwide are multifaceted. You can volunteer to help in project development or jump into an already self-running program in schools and orphanages in many areas of Africa, like Ghana and Sierra Leone. The children forced into making chocolate to feed our need never get to taste the products of their slave labor. Volunteer to help stop this cruel practice and take a bit of bitterness out of these sweets.

BEST PLACES TO TEACH ENGLISH ABROAD

HOMEBRED AMERICANS,

Brits, and Aussies have a skill that's in high demand in many parts of the world: English. Your native language is pretty much The Man when it comes to business, education, and foreign affairs, and the need for English-language teachers is higher than the supply. Some language-based volunteering opportunities focus on teaching kids, while others are all about adults. Either way, the experiences you'll gain being the head honcho of a classroom will look good on your résumé and feel great in the soul.

China

The world's fastest-growing economy wants native English speakers like MSG wants noodles, and the swelling market ensures competitive salaries and great perks. As could be expected, certification regulation isn't terribly stringent—a Bachelor's degree is usually enough. Respectful students and community-oriented people will help to temper the cultural shock and send you home with some bones in your pocket at the end of the school year. Check out the English Teaching Program in Shenzhen (ChinaProgram.org) and the Council on International Education Exchange (Ciee.org).

South Korea

Riding high on the Asiatic TEFL/ESL boom, teaching English at one of many South Korean gigs offers perks like free accommodations, insurance benefits, and return airfare. Contracts usually last for a year, and the low cost of living outside of ultra-modern Seoul affords plenty of time to save up a respectable salary. Be warned: you'll need to brush up on regional cultural norms before you go because Korean social etiquette can be a bit tricky. South Korea boasts the world's highest-estimated national IQ and the most sophisticated IT infrastructure on the planet. So bring the smarts, hard. You can rest assured it's legit: the Korean government has introduced English program initiatives such as English Program in Korea (EPIK) and Teach and Learn in Korea (TALK).

Czech Republic

Though you'll have to apply for a special work visa if you're not one of those lucky EU passport-holding bastards, teaching in the Czech Republic is your ticket to history's playground. There's a super-tight expat community here, and the beer is literally cheaper than water. If you're looking for a place with plenty of weekend-trip opportunities, you've hit gold—the country is landlocked by Germany, Poland, Slovakia, and Austria. Prague is where the party's at, but if cultural immersion is what you're after, consider teaching in a smaller town such as Plzeň or Brno. The weekly English-language newspaper, *The Prague Post*, is a good source to browse while looking for jobs from home. Check out TEFL Worldwide Prague (TeflWorldwidePrague.com) for additional information.

Turkey

In the interest of being straight-up, you're not going to make megabucks here. But the country's ancient heritage and mix of international influence casts a spell on Westerners. We're talkin' ridiculous architecture, delicious grub, and gorgeous people. The Turkish middle class is eager to speak our language, and there are plenty of TEFL/ESL opportunities. Istanbul is pricey, so scoping out gigs in smaller cities is your best bet. No matter where you go, you'll be in the land of Turkish baths and the geographical wonders of Kapadokya and Ölüdeniz. For job postings, keep an eye on *Turkey Daily News* and

Craigslist Istanbul. Try your luck with the English Centre, a language institute in Istanbul and online resources such as My Merhaba and Expat in Turkey.

Kyrgyzstan

Stray from the typical teaching curriculum, and land on the roof of the world—Central Asia remains virtually untouched by the tourism boom. Kyrgyzstan is the easiest country in Central Asia to enter with a Western passport, has a young capital (Bishkek), and is rich in nomadic culture. Though the city doesn't have much to offer by way of history, it has a bright nightlife and enough bars to pump you full of all the antifreeze you'll need to get through a Kyrgyz winter. Nearly entirely blanketed by the mighty Tien Shan mountain range, the country offers some awesome trekking, horseback riding, and camping adventures. The Kyrgyz are known for their hospitality, but be prepared: they also have a strange penchant for Chinese food and karaoke. The London School in Bishkek (TheLondonSchool.org) offers TEFL jobs. As a foreign teacher, you'll get free accommodations and be paid fortnightly (a little foreign-speak for you).

Before you start packing your bags, make sure you've done your research. Your contract should be transparent in terms of duration, duties and compensation, and you need to read it closely. You don't want to be blindsided by a situation where you're stuck longer than you want, or get into more than you signed up for. Teaching abroad isn't just about making money or having the ability to wander longer. You're fueling the future by filling in-demand voids.

NANNIES, MANNIES, AND MARY POPPINS: HOW TO WORK AS AN AU PAIR ABROAD

IF YOUR ONLY BABY EXPERI-ence is playing peek-a-boo with your cousin's kid at Thanksgiving, forget about it. Blubbery mini-humans expel shit (and other foul goo) that's not worth the time unless you're an experienced, cheek-pinching baby enthusiast—and if you are, the juice is worth the squeeze. You can easily learn the basics of a language from a toddler and go places with the family that you'd never be able to afford to see on your own. Europe and Singapore are popular destinations and the British Jobs Abroad Bulletin is your go-to site. Great Au Pair has listings

for au pairs, babysitters, pet sitters, house sitters, senior caretakers, and tutors. Not a job for nomads, but if you're planning on settling down for a while, you can make mad money watching rugrats.

Where to Pair?

Some countries (like Belgium) have strict regulations on non-EU au pairs. Italians tend to take their au pairs on summer vacation and pay a little more for their services. Germans and the French prefer longer-term au pairs (six to twelve months) and require basic language skills in the host language. Native English-speaking au pairs are in high demand in Spain, and it's one of the best bets for easy job placement.

Creds

If you want to stand out in a sea of nanny wannabes, make sure you've logged some hours babysitting at home with a formal agency that can write you a reference. Some countries and agencies require 200 hours of sitting before they'll consider taking you onboard. Brush up on your skills in the language of the country of your choice so you can at least babble with the babies (and understand your hosts!). Ditch your smoking habit while you're at it—while you might end up in a smoking household, you're more appealing to potential employers if you can check the nonsmoker box. First-Aid certification is essential.

Mannies

These days, mannies (or male nannies) are all the rage with the enlightened set. While there's still some hesitation in many places on letting the guys in on the kid fun, more agencies these days are accepting male applicants, particularly ones that place au pairs in France. And chicks dig dudes who are awesome with kids.

If you love watching *Blue's Clues* in a foreign language and chillin' with pint-sized poopers, then get into the au pair game. You'll learn a language, have a roof over your head, and earn party money for your days off (and breath-mint money for your days on).

PLAYING GAMES, CHANGING LIVES

YOUR GLORY DAYS OF HIGH school speedball domination may be long gone, but playing (and owning at) sports will forever live on. For all you gym-class-heroes-turned-vagabond-supertramps, volunteer organizations worldwide offer opportunities to live in foreign lands, play games, and change the lives of poverty-stricken kids on a daily basis.

Kabul, Afghanistan

During Osama bin Laden's cave-jumping days, Kabul got bombed and shred to pieces as part of the search. Today, Afghanistan's largest city is still recovering, and the youth of the nation are often forgotten amidst all the chaos. Rather than waiting for the next bomb to drop, a group of international skaters got together and started Skateistan (Skateistan.org), a skateboarding school in Kabul where displaced local kids not only learn to skate, but also get instruction in language, arts, and civic responsibility. Kickflip your volunteer career into action here with Skateistan, and they'll cover all of your expenses (from flights to food) over a six-month stint.

Transylvania, Romania

True that Transylvania is decorated with creepy castles, but it also packs hike-friendly mountains and beachside resorts. Romania has been free from communism since 1989, but this now-capitalist country could still use your help. Physical education is brushed aside throughout schooling, so more and more volunteer organizations are popping up to fill the gap. Your workweek will be split up between teaching and playing whichever sports you'd like at various orphanages, centers for disabled children, and daycare centers for economically disadvantaged children—all of which seek out ablebodied and fun-spirited volunteers regularly.

Accra, Ghana

Formerly known as the Gold Coast and famous for its friendly inhabitants, the English-speaking country of Ghana is situated on Africa's West Coast. Politically stable and safe, Ghana is one of the best places in which to experience your first African adventure; it's filled with beaches, offers safari tours, and boasts dense rainforests. The gold and cocoa plantations were once profitable enough to build a kingdom for the Ashanti (Ghana's largest tribe), but the country as a whole is terribly poor. Still, in 2006, Ghana kicked some serious ass in the World Cup, and the popularity of soccer in the country has since surged. Through the sports coaching programs of Cosmic Volunteers (CosmicVolunteers.org), you can spend between one and three weeks of your summer as a soccer coach or camp counselor, helping enthusiastic kids reach their superstar potentials. The love of basketball is also creeping into the country, and similar opportunities are available.

HUMAN RIGHTS

THE SAD TRUTH ABOUT THE WORLD IS THAT NOT EVERYONE is granted even basic human rights. In many countries, social class, race, and gender play a large factor in the uneven distribution of rights. Whether your interest lies in helping women find freedom from sexual oppression or narrowing the gaps between social classes by volunteering in education, many international organizations, like Peace Corps, exist to help you fight the good fight, all while further fueling your travels.

ALL ABOUT THE PEACE CORPS

THE PEACE CORPS WAS

created in 1961 to promote world peace and friendship by offering the helping hands of Americans to countries in need. Hundreds of thousands of volunteers have since served in over a hundred different countries. Since the organization is so well established—and pretty selective— being a Peace Corps volunteer has become a rite of passage and an excellent résumé builder for anyone interested in a career in global development. A two-year stint in a foreign country with travel, food, and living expenses all taken care of does sound pretty sweet. But it isn't all peaceful hand-holding and love hugs. We'll shake down everything about this government-run program so you can better see if you want to climb up the Peace Corps tree.

The Mission

The agency asks for twenty-seven months of your time: three for in-country training on language, cross-cultural, technical, and health skills, and the remaining twenty-four for spending in an appointed host country, fulfilling your duties. In return, they'll pay for your travel to and from the country, cover medical and dental expenses during service, provide you with living quarters, and give you a monthly allowance large enough to cover food, and other fun stuff. On top of that, you get a nice chunk of change (currently $7,425 before taxes) when your service is complete. As a Peace Corps volunteer, you can try your helpful hand at educating the world's youth; creating shelters, jobs, and opportunities; and keeping the planet green.

Application Process

There are six separate fields in the program, and all emphasize education. You can apply for specific positions in Education; Health and HIV/AIDS; Business and Information and Communication Technology; Environment, Youth and Community Development; and Agriculture. As long as you're an of-age U.S. citizen you can apply, but since getting accepted has become fairly competitive, at least some background (college degree, prior experience, etc.) in a designated field will make you a much more appealing candidate. Jobs cycle fast, and the process takes months so get on it quick if you're game.

Downsides

In theory, the Peace Corps is a fantastic agency set out to better the world. In practice, many people have found their service to be a bit sketchy at times. Not all communities welcome wide-eyed Americans with open arms, and many have their own preconceived notions about our culture (or lack thereof). Manage your expectations, and—like you always should when traveling—stay alert.

Many places that need help from the Peace Corps need it for a reason. They can be dangerous, unstructured, lawless lands, and as a Peace Corps Volunteer (PVC), it's up to you to stay tight on your shit. Volunteers have had their gear stolen, gotten sick throughout their service, fought with locals who sometimes aren't as friendly as you'd imagine, and—the Peace Corps' largest looming problem—women have been raped. Worst of all, among these unforeseeable issues, is that the Peace Corps isn't always as responsive as you'd hope. Try to envision twenty-seven months of service before you sign up, 'cause it'll be a long time until you'll be back home dreaming about traveling again.

The Peace Corps definitely has its ups and downs. It won't exactly be fun or easy, but the best experiences never are. Some days will be long and grueling; others will be positively life-changing—for you and those in your community.

The Haps with Habitat

HABITAT FOR HUMANITY IS A CHRISTIAN ORGANIZATION THAT'S been at the forefront of building housing for those in need since the mid-'70s. Initially, Habitat aimed to build affordable housing for low-income Americans through the use of donated funds and labor. In 1984, former president Jimmy Carter participated in a building program in NYC, which gave the organization a PR boost and caused Habitat's popularity to skyrocket. With the help of volunteers, they have built over half a million homes worldwide. You don't have to believe in Noah and his ark to volunteer your biceps, strength, and hammering skills. International programs run from six months to a year and are available in countries all over the world.

SEX SELLS SLAVES

ALL TASSELS AREN'T CREA-
ted equal. There are currently nearly thirty million slaves in the modern "free" world—more than at any other time in history. Thriving off of the reality that "sex sells," human trafficking is a severe, global atrocity that still goes largely unnoticed, despite the fact that it takes place in plain view. Fortunately, there are many ways to be part of the solution, beginning with learning about the situation.

The Issue

The human sex trade is a $32-billion-dollar per year business. Simply stated, slavery continues to exist because of greed and poverty. Sex is a profitable market, second only to illegal drugs, with many "business-men" dipping into both sex and drugs to double the financial gain. Like any sharp businessmen, human traffickers gauge their industry and pounce on opportunity. Wherever there is an extreme tragedy forcing victims into homelessness, or desperation (like the earthquake in Haiti), there are lurking predators waiting in the wings to offer "assistance." Promising the poor and hungry a chance to eat and make money, these scumbag traffick-ers lure downtrodden women into working in brothels, massage parlors, and strip clubs, or onto the streets where they work off their "debts." Most of the victims are women under the age of eighteen. Many are chil-dren who are handed over by their own parents—who are tricked into believing that they are sending their kid to learn a legitimate trade that will eventually bring money into the household. Human trafficking is prevalent wherever there is poverty, especially throughout Southeast Asia, Africa, India, Eastern Europe, and South America.

Giving Women Real Choices

Numerous organizations are attempting to abolish modern slavery by empowering victims with tools to financially sustain themselves and their families, providing them alter-natives to selling their bodies to sur-vive. Various organizations are work-ing toward a solution by providing a space for women to sell their hand-made items and showcase their other skills. Imani (ImaniLove.com) sells beautiful, handcrafted jewelry made by Ugandan women who are victims of sexual slavery. The women are paid fair wages to make jewelry from indigenous materials and are also offered business and English courses, as well as counseling to fuel their recovery and lead them to the road of freedom. Other organizations like Not For Sale are partnering with sister groups around the globe to set up job-training programs for human-trafficking victims. These programs also offer safe shelter, holistic healing classes, and day care to help victims transition.

Ways You Can Help

It is important to remember that, without demand, there is no need for supply. We're not suggesting that you never go to a strip club again, but disengaging yourself from the activities that perpetuate the problem will lessen the demand. Sex tourism in places like Thailand encourages people to travel to certain destinations solely for the opportunity to meet underage girls and boys. If something seems creepy, it probably is—hands off! There are hundreds of hands-on ways to get involved in the movement to end modern slavery. If you fancy yourself a writer or designer, contact one of the many organizations like Not For Sale and donate your talent and time. Next time you have a gift to buy in countries where sex trafficking is prevalent, seek out items handmade by women and make purchases with a purpose.

Prostitution and stripping are not always tied to modern slavery. Women often make an educated, empowered choice to participate in these professions, and there's nothing wrong with that. But for those whose "choice" is a life or death situation, their bodies and lives are no longer their own. As backpackers who are shamelessly into tits and ass, we need to be aware of this dehumanizing atrocity and start becoming part of the solution. No effort is too small, except no effort at all.

WILL WORK FOR FOOD

WHILE EVERYONE'S INTER-pretation of what makes a good meal varies culturally, one thing is universal across the board: we all need to eat. The problem is, over a billion people around the world don't (and can't), due to factors like lack of access to adequate food sources, droughts, natural disasters, or civil conflicts. The benefits of dropping off a bowl of rice and beans (an approach taken by some relief organizations) are short-lived, and volunteer programs are often too temporary to make a real difference. Building your career around alleviating world hunger—now that's a tasty idea that sits well in the stomach.

Get Your Creds

Devoting your life to combating hunger starts with getting a degree in the field. The main umbrella for this sort of work is known as International Development, and you can study the field at all levels (BA, MA, and PhD). If you want to get more specific, there are programs that go into the economics of food scarcity and security, agricultural development, nutrition, and logistics (moving food from developed to developing countries), among others.

Start Small

If you like getting down and dirty, there are plenty of opportunities to work directly with local communities on a smaller scale. If you want to be outdoors, check into small sustainable farms that need help with planting, reaping seasonal harvests, and transporting food to markets. Working at food banks (both at home and abroad) will usually put you in direct contact with those who need a helping hand. If you're obsessed with food documentaries and read books like *The Omnivore's Dilemma*, put all of that food knowledge to use and teach nutrition classes in communities that have high rates of malnutrition. If fair trade is your game, find organizations that advocate for fair wages paid to small farmers in exchange for their quality produce.

Fuck It, Go Big!

An industry giant, the United Nations' World Food Programme is first to respond when disasters strike and wipe out food sources. These guys also work to prepare for emergencies before they happen, as well as educate communities worldwide on nutrition and agriculture. Another huge NGO (non-governmental organization) that dominates the field is the Food and Agriculture Organization (FAO) of the United Nations. The FAO focuses on everything from sustainable farming practices to researching water scarcities. Both organizations are constantly looking for internationally-minded individuals with varied skills and offer opportunities that place employees and interns on projects all around the world. Pick up some creds working in the field and apply to the opportunities these big shots have available.

SUSTAINABILITY

IT'S NO SECRET THAT OUR WORLD IS IN CRISIS ECOLOGICALLY. While sorting your recycling and refusing plastic bags is a good start, if you're passionate about sustainability, your time can be better spent digging your hands into environmental issues abroad. Working on sustainability projects, in many cases, will be a chance to escape the big cities and learn about the local culture from the ground up. By picking your own dinner on an organic farm or fighting pollution on a Greenpeace boat, you'll be helping sustain the planet for generations of backpackers to come.

GET ON THE GREENPEACE BOAT!

YOU'VE SURELY HEARD OF

the world-changing force that is Greenpeace, but did you know it all started with a boat? In the '70s, when shit was shaky, a few Canadian hippies got on a boat to Amchitka, Alaska, in hopes of peacefully rolling through to stop U.S. nuclear testing in the area. In true hippie fashion, the money to fund the voyage came from a concert headlined by Joni Mitchell, which sold out and raked in a good chunk of change for the cause. The voyage was both a failure and a success. While the U.S. navy stopped the hippie ship dead in the water, the awareness that their bold actions brought inspired the formation of an organization that would change the face of the world, one environmental issue at a time.

Today, the "meet them head-on" mission is still alive and flowing through the organization's green veins. Headquartered in Amsterdam, Greenpeace organizes activists around the world to address issues like deforestation in the Amazon, sustainable agriculture, toxic pollution, and saving the Arctic. You can volunteer in your local community or at their headquarters (if you have a Dutch work visa or EU passport, that is), donate some dollars, or raise awareness online. All good and great, but if you've got a little sailing experience under your belt, Greenpeace offers three-month, paid stints on their muthafuckin' boats!

Sticking to the original mode of activist transport, Greenpeace has a fleet of ships, including inflatable boats with super-fast engines that they use to roll up on trouble. The fleet includes The Rainbow Warrior, The Arctic Sunrise, The Esperanza, and The Argus, and all of the ships are refurbished to be completely eco-friendly and safe. Past missions have included actions against nuclear testing, offshore oil drilling, and toxic dumping. In addition, Greenpeace conducts various eco studies aboard their ships, sailing to locations all around the world to collect data. If your sea legs are wobbly, they also have hot air balloons that hold up to three people and occasionally drift around campaigning for clean air.

To apply for a ship job online, you must either have some experience and valid STCW-95 license *or* convince them that you're too awesome to pass up in 2,500 words or less.

Odd Jobs to Fund Your Travels

FREEDOM ISN'T FREE. LEAVING
The Man behind may have been the reason for your trip, but he's still out there—lurking in every corner of the world—demanding that you pay up. With work visas and employment restrictions, you can't simply slap on a suit and tie and sell your soul for a little dough on the road. But don't worry. There are plenty of ways to boost that bank account while you're livin' the life—and none of them require paperwork or government approval.

Get Crafty
Making cool shit and selling it on the street is the most popular way backpackers keep the cash flow positive. The possibilities are endless, and you don't need much capital to get started. You can eat for weeks by making necklaces and earrings from shells, discarded wire, and pretty river stones. Stock up on string and hooks in a big city. But be warned: in certain countries or cities it might be illegal or even require a permit to sell products or collect shells, so be sure to do your research first!

Go Green
European festivals are breeding grounds for cold, hard cash. In many countries, like Germany, you can trade in plastic bottles for moola. Most festival-goers are too stoned to worry about where they leave their recycling—consequently, surrounding campgrounds become treasure troves of plastic bottles waiting to be traded for cash.

Tried and True
Offering your own sweat and blood is the oldest trick in the book, and it works like a charm. Many hostels need an extra pair of hands in the kitchen or bar, and will offer you a free bed and/or cheap food in exchange. It's a prime gig for meeting people—who doesn't want to cozy up to the bartender?

Get Gnarly
Ali Baba pants aside, dreadlocks are the ultimate in backpacker chic. If you can make 'em, you've got guaranteed work in the traveler's community from Fiji to France. Depending on where you are, you can get more than $100 a head—especially in beach towns. Pack a couple of metal crocheting needles and a dog comb, and then watch some YouTube tutorials to give yourself a dread-ucation.

Kick It and Flip It
If circumventing the globe is in your travel plan, with a little forethought, this gig makes fiscal sense. While chilling in cheaper countries, like India or Thailand, stock up on cool, lightweight hippie shit. When you make it to the other side of the world, sell it at street fairs or festivals.

BURNERS WITHOUT BORDERS (BWB)

"BURNERS" ARE REGULAR

attendees of the Burning Man Project—a weeklong, communal utopian festival that takes place in a Nevada "playa" for one week at the end of every August. Describing Burning Man to someone who has never gone is like explaining yellow to the color-blind. But just to give you an idea: start with a wild, mind-boggling array of costumes, art cars, sound camps, and massive exhibits, all provided by the self-reliant community. Insert a group of Burners tripping, rolling, bumping, dropping, and puffing—pretty much everything a fat kid does in gym class—and smatter it all with looooove, and you've got a peek into the phenomenon. Burning Man festival is a tripped-out week of debauch-

ery and creativity in the desert, and the visuals that come out of it are reminiscent of the things that make Hunter S. Thompson iconic to our generation. Add a bit of Mother Teresa's do-gooder mentality to that to create Burners without Borders (BWB), an organization that is dedicated to creatively approach world issues. BWB began in 2005 when a group of Burners helped rebuild several New Orleans communities ravaged by Hurricane Katrina. The idea caught fire, and the organization now travels across the globe to lead grassroots campaigns in desperate areas where all other aid has failed.

Pisco Sin Fronteras (PSF)—Pisco, Peru

In 2007, an 8.0 earthquake threatened to wipe the coastal town of Pisco, Peru, off the map. International aid poured in, but then many aid groups hitched a ride with the camera crews on their way out of town. Pisco Sin Fronteras ("Pisco without Borders") is BWB's first international offshoot and is still going strong. Their projects include rebuilding the city's infrastructure (homes, sanitation, schools), promoting community involvement, preserving and restoring the environment, and even producing their own biodiesel fuel. PSF is looking for skilled volunteers but just like on the playa, they'll welcome anyone who cares with a great big hug.

Eco-Pesa— Mombasa, Kenya

Life in Mombasa's Kongowea slum was pretty destitute, and there was little hope for improvement. Local businesses took in about $5 a day, could not get a loan, and could not afford to hire from the huge number of unemployed people. Donations that came into the community flowed directly out of it, leaving little currency and trade within Kongowea. A lack of social services, like waste management, made things even slummier. Burners without Borders developed an ingenious economic model to promote local businesses and beautify the slum by printing a local currency for use only within Kongowea. The "Eco-Pesa" is backed by, and pegged to, the Kenyan shilling and was introduced to seventy-five local "Eco-Businesses" at a discounted rate. The exclusive currency kept trade locked inside of Kongowea. Donations were converted to Eco-Pesa and used to pay kids for

trash collection, tree planting, community service, and anything else that would help turn the community from a craphole into a place worth living. The Eco-Pesa could then only be spent within the community, generating more local business. Finally, low-interest Eco-Pesa loans were distributed to small, eco-friendly businesses. The program has proven to be successful and has since expanded to other slums of the city. Volunteers are needed as they look to replicate the model elsewhere in Kenya and abroad.

Greening the Beige— Beijing, China

"Beige" is as much a take on the city name as it is a description of the thick haze that has its inhabitants in a constant chokehold. The smog is so bad that it frequently forces the cancellation of outdoor school activities and is known to ground flights. Twenty million Beijingers don't even realize this is fucked. The government calls it a "fog," and access to the outside world is blocked by the Great (fire) Wall of China. The challenge wasn't overwhelming enough to deter a group of Burners, though. The small, free-spirited operation has been promoting environmental awareness through the arts since 2007. Exhibits and competitions use recycled materials to engage and educate the Beijing community about conservation and sustainability. In an effort to clear the air, Greening the Beige encourages ideas from volunteers that explore the project's endless creative potential.

WWOOF, WWOOF, BABY!

WWOOFING DOESN'T REFER to barking but stands for "World Wide Opportunities on Organic Farms"-ing. This network (WWOOF) was developed to link volunteers to organic farms with available volunteer opportunities. You volunteer on an international farm for an agreed amount of hours, and they feed and house your hungry, broke ass. Pretty fair deal. Nothing extravagant here, but given the prices of organic, fresh-from-the-ground food and housing, it's a good trade-off.

The Production Problem

Unfortunately, the factory farming method of meat production in the United States is spreading its long arm overseas. By now, you have all seen the hidden camera videos of animals on large farms being abused and neglected, and of chickens with breasts so large that their legs break, cramped in tiny spaces to maximize production. Our cows are diseased, pigs are electrocuted, and turkeys are strangled, and all in the name of producing the millions of burgers, nuggets, and what-nots we're all so attached to.

When animals become commodities and farms are replaced by factories, humane methods of raising and slaughtering animals are compromised to turn higher profits. In response, some have chosen to become vegetarians, while others have deferred their hard-earned cash to more expensive organic, free-range meat and dairy options. The sad truth is that small, humane, family-owned farms are struggling to compete. Being a vegetarian, vegan, or organic/free-range meat-eater is a statement; rolling up your sleeves and actually getting down and dirty at a farm is putting your statement into action.

Ya'll City Folk? No Problem

No farming experience is necessary to wwoof with the best of them. Daily duties range from milking cows to plowing, sowing, maintaining animal sheds, and planting seeds. This work will be hard, and you will get that ugly farmer's tan, but your contribution will be greatly appreciated and rewarded.

Even if you couldn't care less about the well-being of animals, by volunteering you get to live in a foreign country of your choice as a farmer (which is the closest you can get to local culture) and escape the tourist traps by living in the countryside. Plus, you get the freshest food available in the region, daily.

How to Start Living Off the Land

Whether you're a vegetarian looking to support small farms or a meat-eater looking for a unique (and damn cheap) way to live and eat abroad, hooking up with a farm through the WWOOF network is a good idea. While your friends back home are eating canned, frozen, and pesticide-covered produce, you'll be holding a fresh, organic vegetable in one hand and a hoe in the other.

1. Wwoofing organizations exist almost everywhere in the world where there is a farm. There is no global membership, but you sometimes have to pay a small, country-specific annual fee (used to maintain the organization) to join the wwoofing network. For instance, the annual fee in Argentina costs $28, but Estonia is free. Go to Wwoof.org, pick a country, pay your fee, and you'll get a list of farms.

2. Choose your ideal farm (animal, fruit and vegetable, grain, or a combination) from the list. Keep in mind the type of work will correlate with the kind of farm you choose. So, if squeezing udders makes you shudder, stick to produce production.

3. Contact the farm to make a volunteer arrangement. Find out about: duration of volunteership, hours of work per day, days of work per week, type of accommodations offered (tent, private/shared room), and proximity of surrounding towns.

4. Get a plane ticket, put on some sunscreen, and get to work.

BOTTLE SCHOOLS

HUG IT FORWARD, A UNITED States-based nonprofit, takes the "Reduce, Reuse, Recycle" mantra to a new level. In 2009, these guys began constructing "bottle schools" from plastic bottles and other trash in Guatemala. Most of the villages where bottle schools are built are rural and poor, often hours from a paved road. Sadly—but also happily—these trashy classrooms are often the first schools the villages have ever had.

Bottle and Mortar

The first step to building a bottle school is to collect thousands of plastic bottles and make them into eco-bricks by stuffing them full of inorganic trash (to prevent the school from rotting.) The frame is built from concrete and iron for strength. Then, the eco-bricks are stacked on top of each other and sandwiched between

chicken wire. A couple layers of cement are slapped on for good measure, and then the building gets its Central American mojo when it's painted in festive colors.

These schools aren't built in a day, or without plenty of lending hands. Serve the World Today, a for-profit company, runs voluntourism trips in coordination with Hug It Forward. By volunteering your time and taking a trip down (with twenty-four other like-minded volunteers), you can do some good for Guatemala.

Plastic with a Purpose

A bottle school is an in-yo-face testimonial to the possibility of local building, even in the most remote or impoverished communities. But there's more than radical eco-construction going on here—building a bottle school cleans a community's bottle-clogged gutters, educates local kids about recycling, and in the end, gives kids a space within which to learn and play. More than fifteen have been built since the program began.

Program Perks

A bottle school trip includes a coffee farm tour, cultural talks, meals prepared by a private cook, and trips to the trippy Mayan ruins at Mixco Viejo and the city of Antigua, a UNESCO World Heritage site. Most importantly, because you'll be working shoulder-to-shoulder with the locals, you'll have the chance to build relationships with both Guatemalans and other volunteers.

A bottle school trip costs around $1,195, which covers everything but your transportation to Guatemala, booze, and souvenirs. Additionally, every bottle school volunteer is asked to fundraise $250 for the project pre-departure. However you decide to do this is up to you, but Hug It Forward has some fun suggestions, and every cent of the money you raise goes directly to a school project. Just like every small piece of trash that eventually constructs a school, it's worth every penny.

WRAPPING UP

WE HOPE THIS BOOK HAS MADE YOU UNCOMFORTABLY anxious to travel, and helped you realize that the material things holding you back are worthless. By no means is this text exhaustive; it is simply a glimpse into the wonderful underworld of travel, filled with street food, art, music, parties, and the opportunity to learn about the world by experiencing the different ways people conceptualize the idea.

On the road, you'll learn that travel is only partially about the destination. Being out of your element—wherever you are in the world—teaches you to tap into your survival skills physically, mentally, and socially. You will figure out valuable lessons about yourself and how you respond to novel situations. Some people you meet will lead lives wildly different from yours, and others will be eerily similar. You will find that friendship is universal; that language barriers are easy to overcome; that no matter how broke you are, there is always a way to get a drink, share a laugh, and dance like you mean business. You will sleep standing up, eat lying down, sprint through airports and bus stations like an Olympic athlete, get thrown off your intended path only to find something much more exciting, discuss political theory using mostly hand gestures and grunts, and love every minute of it.

When clicking through other people's travel photos just won't cut it anymore, we urge you to start planning a trip of your own. Before you get bogged down with student loans, mortgages, kids, spouses, and responsibilities, learn a little about yourself by hitting the road. You don't need much money to have the time of your life abroad, as long as you decide that comfort can wait, that food tastes better street-side, and that being a little grimy isn't a big deal. Sacrifice to disappear, and the world becomes yours.

THE AUTHORS

COFOUNDER Anna Starostinetskaya

Anna was born in Ukraine, raised in Los Angeles, and currently resides in Brooklyn, New York. Her most memorable trip was to Spain, where she hopped a fence on the side of a highway to sample an authentic Spanish olive right from a tree. Don't eat olives from trees for two reasons: (1) they have not been cured and taste like utter shit, and (2) if the grove's owner catches you trespassing, you may leave Spain with more battle wounds than you intended.

Brian Biros

Brian is a certifiable travel-fiend. His contributions to this book were formulated from a hammock in Ecuador. He has traveled the world twice, called over 200 hostels home, slept on several dozen couches, was busted for smuggling gypsies into Germany, chugged a beer at the summit of Mt. Kilimanjaro, was bitch slapped by a manta ray, and lived to tell (you) about it.

Christopher Platis

Chris is originally from Greece, one of the sexiest places around. He recently spent some time bruising his tidbits in Switzerland and schmoozing his way into Berlin's clubs and art scene. When he's not writing for OTP, Chris puts in solid research at some of New York and New Jersey's finest beaches.

Lisette Cheresson

Skipping the seas and spreading her word seed, Lisette is a Brooklyn-based writer, filmmaker, and adventuress. If you feel like feeding monkeys in South America or getting naked on the Great Wall of China, she's your go-to gal for advice.

Sara M. White

A little sweet, a little sour, and a whole lotta spicy, Sara is a quirky ball of travel-writing genius. She spent some time studying theater and dance in Bali, and has taught English in Thailand. While most people would love to brag about just riding an elephant, not only did this girl mount the beast for a gallop, but she also bathed it for extra credit. She's an over-achiever; we like that.

Sarah Binion

Sarah is happiest when she's sitting on a train, reading Paul Theroux while simultaneously drinking wine and coffee. Her favorite journey by rail was aboard the Dacia Express between Bucharest and Vienna. When she's not dousing herself in beverages aboard the world's finest trains, she divides her time between London, Austin, and New Orleans.

EXECUTIVE DIRECTOR/ COFOUNDER
Freddie Pikovsky

The ringmaster of OTP, Freddie fell in love with backpacking on a trip in 2009 that started in Israel; went through Greece, Italy, Spain, France, and the Netherlands; and ended in travel enlightenment. He often travels in a style known as "broke fancy," which has landed him in some precarious situations. Once calling the floor of an Italian train station home for the night, Freddie came close to being swept away by a street-cleaning truck as he snoozed comfortably on pizza crumbs and petrified gum. He's a firm believer that every young person should experience the life-changing capabilities of travel and drives OTP forward to make this vision a reality.

SPECIAL THANKS TO:

Adil Dara Kim
Bianca Rappaport
Connie Nguyen
Erin Ridley
Jaclyn Einis
Kyle McNichols
Lorenzo R. Ramos
Mark Ayling
Taveeshi Singh
Timothy Melough
Photo Editor: Tiffany Pilgrim
Adam Silver
Rishe Groner

THIS BOOK WOULD NOT

have been possible without the people who have supported our mission throughout our journey. Thank you to all of you who have contributed your talents, advice, and good vibes along the way.

INDEX

PHOTO CREDITS

p. 10: William Alphonsus Butler, Masterbutler.tumblr.com; p. 14: J Brew "brewbooks"; p. 15: Siri Schwartzman; p. 16 and end papers: Sascha Grabow, Saschagrabow.com; p. 17 and end papers: Aviachar Avinash Achar; p. 19: Mark Dumont (#1), Pardee Ave. (#2), Anna J. Phillips, Renzo Arauco-Brown, Alejandro Oceguera-Figueroa, Gloria P. Gomez, María Beltrán, Yi-Te Lai, Mark E. Siddall (#3), April Nobile (#4), Cl.udio Dias Timm (#5); p. 20 and end papers: BiblioArchives/LibraryArchives; p. 21: Mack Male; p. 22: Andrew Purdam; p. 23: José Antonio Morcillo Valenciano (top and end papers), TheDoGoodDames (middle); p. 24: The Adventurists (top), Travelchat.co.za (bottom); p. 25: Vinoth Chandar; p. 26: Philip Larson; p. 27: GaudiAZ (top, bottom, and end papers); p. 28 and end papers: NeilsPhotography, Neilsrtw.blogspot.com; p. 29: "karlnorling," Jno.se/; p. 31: JorgeBRAZIL; p. 32 and end papers: Ipoh kia; p. 33: Andrew Bowden (top), Mark "Strenqth" (bottom); p. 34: Duncan Brown (Cradlehall); p. 35: Warren Rohner; p. 36: Chris Martin; p. 37 and end papers: Richard Giddins; p. 39: Alex Goldmark (middle left), Lesley Unruh - Creativity-online.com (middle top), Crane/Sand - Gluesociety.com (middle bottom); p. 40: "claumoho"; p. 41: Laura Padgett (bottom left), Radamantis Torres (bottom right); p. 42 and end papers: Meindert van D; p. 43: Rob Shenk (top), Alex Torrenegra (bottom); p. 44 and end papers: Carolyn Conner; p. 45: Ira Mowen (top and end papers); b.frahm (bottom); p. 46 and end papers: Gino Zabala Bianchi; p. 47: Gino Zabala Bianchi (top), Viviaan A. (bottom and end papers); p. 48 and end papers: beccafrog; p. 49: Robert S. Digby (top), David Stanley (bottom); p. 50: herval; p. 51 and end papers: Karen Green; p. 52: JJ & Special K (top), Rob React (middle), DJ Philly G (bottom); p. 53: Christian Cortes (top left and end papers) "Underdestruction" (top right and end papers), Salim Virji (middle), NYCUrbanScape - Peter Cigliano (bottom and end papers); p. 54: Jules Antonio; p. 55: "indy_slug" (top), Tim Fuller (bottom); p. 56: Mauro "Kilamdil" Monti (top), "bixentro" (bottom and end papers); p. 57 and end papers: Moyan Brenn; p. 58: Jean-Pierre Dalbéra; p. 59: Jean-Pierre Dalbéra (top), "Renegat" (middle and end papers); p. 61: Adam Silver (#1), Jeff Smith (#2), Claude

Peddington (#3), Freddie Pikovsky (#4), Don Kramer (#5); p. 62: Jorge from Tokyo; p. 64: Christian Lau; p. 65: Toby Oxborrow; p. 69: "cute as heck" (top), David Berkowitz (bottom); p. 70: "apparent"; p. 72: "Yenkassa"; p. 74: Christian Van Der Henst S.; p. 75: April Killingsworth (left), Freddie Pikovsky (right); p. 76: stu_spivack; p. 77: "spine186"; p. 78: TheGirlsNY — Kim (top), "Loozrboy" (bottom); p. 79: Icelandenquirer.blogspot.com; p. 80: "Lil Wolf"; p. 82: Richard @ Ladyous.blogspot.com; p. 83: Visitingeu.com (top), Yun Huang Yong (bottom); p. 84: "Yoshi"; p. 85: Agostino Fedeli; p. 86: rugbyxm, Ryan Erickson; p. 87: "Kudo Momo"; p. 88: Sara Goldsmith (top and end papers), Michael Voelker (bottom); p. 89: Caryl Joan Estrosas; p. 90: Joseph A Ferris III (top), Neil Simmons (bottom); p. 92: Elizabeth Burnett; pp. 94, 95, and end papers: Jamie Bel-lal; p. 97: Chris "Effervescing"; p. 98: Vyacheslav Argenberg; p. 99: Hunter Desportes (top), "Yo Pizza" (bottom and end papers); p. 101: Matt Corks; p. 102: chromewaves, Frank Yang; p. 104: Dominic Simpson; p. 105: Team at Carnaval.com Studios; p. 106: Brazil Women's Beach Volleyball Team (left and end papers), Marek Krzystkiewicz (right and end papers); p. 107: Xristoforos aka Shooting Dog; p. 108: "krigud"; p. 110: Yun Huang Yong (top), Rose of Academe (middle); p. 112: Mazarias Antoranz (top), Greg -ssy (bottom); p. 113: Peter DeWit; p. 114: Robert Rybnikar (left), Anthony Booker (right); p. 115: Umesh Bansal; p. 116: William Alphonsus Butler, Masterbutler.tumblr.com; p. 121: Jurgen "300tdorg"; p. 122: Hamed Saber; p. 124: Dominic Rivard; p. 125: Staff Sgt. Russell Lee Klika, US Army National Guard; p. 127: "Reinis" (top), garryknight, Garry Knight (bottom and end papers); p. 129: LollyKnit; p. 132: Patrick Yodarus; p. 137: diesel_travis, Travis Hardiman; p. 138: macgodbrad, "bclinesmith"; p. 142: jdklub, Justin Klubnik; p. 146 and end papers: MRGT, Margot Gabel; p. 147 and end papers: Jeremy Brooks; p. 149: chem7 (middle), jwalsh, Jason Walsh (bottom and end papers); p. 151 and end papers: jbozanowski, Jakub Bozanowski; p. 160: aljazeeraenglish, Al Jazeera Newspaper; p. 163: ITSpeaks, Wikimedia Commons; p. 167: Charles Dyer; p. 170: TELO Project; p. 173 and end papers: Holi Drunk@Mumbai, "hermesmerana"; p. 174: ©Corbis; p. 177: shizhao, Shi Zhao; p. 179: Liam Quinn (top), Nathan Johnson (bottom); p. 182: DFID - UK Department for International Development; p. 185: Ton Rulkens; p. 186: Augapfel, Christopher Billman; p. 188 and end papers: "zapstratosphere"; p. 190: Children's Organization of Southeast Asia;

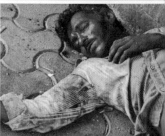